'A fascinating new book . . . Ryan has succeeded in illuminating the sheer diversity of human experiences in 1916, and in particular has highlighted the role of women in the Rising'

Diarmaid Ferriter, Village

'an entertaining book that gives us an insight into the way some of the ordinary people involved in the Easter Rising recalled that experience forty years later. Their voices come through with a lively immediacy that is very attractive.'

History Ireland

'A remarkable new book'

Irish Independent

'an intriguing survey of a fascinating and historically very important Irish archive; a real eye-opener'

Tom Garvin, Irish Book Review

'the accounts bring events alive with an immediacy and sense of location that a more formal history cannot provide . . . [and] help add depth to our understanding of what happened in that fateful week'

Tony Canavan, Books Ireland

'Ms Ryan does reveal many hitherto unsung people who played their part [in the Rising]. She highlights the outstanding women of the Citizen Army. . . . Ms Ryan's memoir is not without humour'

Peter de Rosa, Evening Herald

'a fascinating collection of memories of the Easter Rising from those who took part or who were observers of the action'

Emigrant Online

'a fascinating book . . . the commentary of the women who were the wives, loves and girlfriends of the key participants enlivens the pages'

Post News: The Journal of An Post

First published in 2005 by
Liberties Press
Guinness Enterprise Centre | Taylor's Lane | Dublin 8 | Ireland
www.libertiespress.com | info@libertiespress.com
+353 (1) 415 1286

Trade enquiries to CMD BookSource
55A Spruce Avenue | Stillorgan Industrial Park | Blackrock | County Dublin
Tel: +353 (1) 294 2560
Fax: +353 (1) 294 2564

ISBN 978-1-905483-70-9

4 6 8 10 9 7 5

A CIP record for this title is available from the British Library.

Cover design by Liam Furlong at space.ie
Set in 11-point Garamond

Printed in Ireland by Colour Books
Unit 105 | Baldoyle Industrial Estate | Dublin 13

WITNESSES
INSIDE THE EASTER RISING

ANNIE RYAN

CONTENTS

5

In memory of my father

Author's Acknowledgements

Grateful thanks to the following: Dr Margaret Mac Curtain and Prof. Donal McCartney, whose help was invaluable; Colette O'Daly of the National Library, whose resources, both personal and professional, were always available; Prof. Risteárd Mulcahy, for granting permission to quote from his his book *Richard Mulcahy: A Family Memoir;* my brother Michael, who read, discussed and informed. My husband Brendan was as ever an unfailing support. I am especially indebted to the staff at the National Archives, and to the custodians of the Military Archives in Cathal Brugha Barracks. A special word of thanks to my publishers, who are truly amazing.

Publishers' Note

All quotations from the Bureau of Military History 1913–21 witness statements are reproduced courtesy of Military Archives, Cathal Brugha Barracks, Rathmines, Dublin 6. Extracts from the witness statements have been reproduced verbatim, with the exception of minor editorial amendments, given in square brackets, and occasional stylistic changes, which have been made silently. (Editorial insertions on the part of those who compiled the archive appear in round brackets.) The publishers would like to thank Military Archives, the UCD Archive Department and the Independent Newspaper Group for granting permission to use photographs from their collections, and Commandant Victor Laing, Commandant Pat Brennan and the staff of the Military Archives, and Seamus Helferty and Orna Somerville of the UCD Archive Department, for their assistance. The extract, used in the Foreword, from Derek Mahon's poem 'A Disused Shed in Co. Wexford', from his *Collected Poems,* is reproduced by permission of The Gallery Press, Loughcrew, Oldcastle, County Meath. Finally, the publishers would like to thank Daibhí Mac Domhnaill for the map that appears on page 9.

Map of Dublin Locations

Associated with the Rising

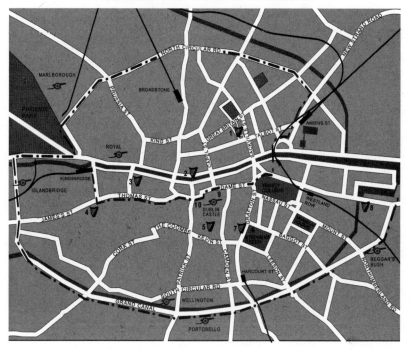

L E G E N D

1 General Post Office
2 The Four Courts
3 Mendicity Institute
4 South Dublin Union
5 Jacob's Factory
6 St Stephen's Green
7 College of Surgeons
8 Boland's Mill
9 Dublin Castle
10 City Hall

Buildings held by rebels

British military bases

British military cordons

0   200m   1000m

GLOSSARY OF ORGANISATIONS

The 1916 Rising had its roots in the 'new nationalism' which emerged in Ireland from the 1890s onwards. Some of the new movements which emerged in this period were mainly cultural, like the GAELIC ATHLETIC ASSOCIATION, founded in 1884 primarily to promote the Gaelic games of football, hurling and handball, and the GAELIC LEAGUE, established by Douglas Hyde and Eoin MacNeill in 1893 to save the Irish language, which at that point was close to extinction. Others were more overtly political. Most of them were infiltrated by the IRISH REPUBLICAN BROTHERHOOD, a small revolutionary body which planned and directed the insurrection of 1916. The revival of this old secret separatist society, which had been active fifty years before, was the most important development in the years immediately preceding the Rising. There follow brief descriptions of some of the most important organisations active around the time of the Rising:

CITIZEN ARMY The Citizen Army, of which Countess Markievicz was a member, was, like the Irish Volunteers, founded in 1913. It was organised and directed by James Connolly and had its origins in the protest rallies of Dublin workers led by James Larkin, founder of the Irish Transport and General Workers Union.

CUMANN NA MBAN Cumann na mBan, a women's league associated with the Irish Volunteers, was founded by Countess Markievicz in association with Agnes O'Farrelly, Jennie Wyse-Power and Louise Gavan Duffy. It had the same aims as the Irish Volunteers but was a separate organisation. As well as learning first aid, the members drilled and learned how to load, unload and clean guns.

FIANNA ÉIREANN Fianna Éireann was founded in 1909 by Countess Markievicz and Bulmer Hobson. Its main aim was to inculcate nationalist principles and to promote the Irish language and Irish culture amongst young men and boys.

HIBERNIAN RIFLES This was a small section of the Ancient Order of Hibernians which was organised by Joseph Scollan in 1911. It was armed and ready for action in 1916. A hundred and fifty Hibernians paraded at the funeral of the Fenian leader O'Donovan Rossa.

INGHINIDHE NA HÉIREANN Inghinidhe na hÉireann was founded in 1900 by Maud Gonne and other women who were active in cultural and political circles. Its aim was 'to combat in every way English influence', which, its members claimed, was 'doing so much injury to artistic taste' in Ireland.

IRISH PARLIAMENTARY PARTY The Irish Parliamentary Party was the dominant force in nationalist politics in Ireland since long before many of the protagonists of the 1916 Rising were born. The party's aspirations towards Home Rule were finally overtaken and sidelined, firstly by the outbreak of the Great War and secondly by the Easter Rising.

IRISH TRANSPORT AND GENERAL WORKERS' UNION The ITGWU was founded in Dublin in 1911 by James Larkin. The union featured in the epic struggle between Dublin workers and employers known as the 1913 Lockout. The ITGWU and other unions was subsumed into SIPTU in recent years.

IRISH VOLUNTEERS This organisation was founded in Dublin in 1913 'to secure the rights and liberties common to all the people of Ireland'. Almost all IRB members were members of the Irish Volunteers as well.

MNA NA HÉIREANN Mna na hÉireann was an early feminist organisation associated with Helena Molony, who consistently advocated equal rights for women.

ROYAL IRISH CONSTABULARY Under British rule, the RIC policed all Ireland. In Dublin, the Dublin Metropolitan Police carried out this function.

SINN FÉIN The foundation of Sinn Féin dates back to 1905. The organisation was an amalgamation of several groups under the influence of Arthur Griffith. It aimed to create 'a prosperous, virile and independent nation'. Griffith advocated a policy of abstention from the Westminster Parliament. Sinn Féin was not directly involved in the Rising.

ULSTER VOLUNTEER FORCE In January 1913, Sir Edward Carson and James Craig set up the Ulster Volunteer Force with the intention of defending Ulster against Home Rule.

DRAMATIS PERSONAE

ROGER CASEMENT (1864–1916) was born in County Dublin. In 1892, he joined the British consular service. He joined the Gaelic League in 1904. He became well know internationally when he exposed the scandalous treatment of indigenous peoples in South America and Africa. In 1911, he was knighted. In 1913, he joined the Irish Volunteers, and he devoted the rest of his life to promoting the movement for Irish independence. In 1916, on landing in Kerry in the *Aud,* he was captured before he could contact the Volunteers and persuade them not to proceed with the Rising. He was hanged on 3 August 1916. He might have escaped the death penalty, had it not been for the fact that the British government had the 'Black Diaries', revealing his homosexuality, circulated.

ÉAMONN CEANNT (1881–1916) Éamonn Ceannt was born in County Galway, the son of an RIC officer. He was a clerk of the Dublin Corporation. He joined the Gaelic League in 1900 and became a member of its governing body, and he was a founder member of the Irish Volunteers. In 1913, he became a member of the IRB; he subsequently became a member of its Supreme Council and Military Council. He was a signatory of the Proclamation of the Irish Republic and a member of the Provisional Government. Ceannt was stationed at the South Dublin Union during the Rising and was executed on 8 May 1916

THOMAS J. CLARKE (1857–1916) Thomas Clarke was born on the Isle of Wight. His mother was from Tipperary, his father from Leitrim; the couple settled in Dungannon, County Tyrone. Clarke emigrated to America and worked in the construction industry in Staten Island. When he was eighteen years of age, he joined the IRB. Shortly afterwards, this organisation sent him to London, where he was captured carrying a case of explosives. He was sentenced to jail and served fifteen years at Pentonville Prison. On his release, he married Kathleen Daly, a niece of John Daly, the mayor of Limerick, who had shared a cell with him at Pentonville. Thomas and Kathleen returned to Ireland, where they set up a small shop in Parnell Street. He later met Sean McDermott, and the two set about reviving the physical-force movement. Clarke's name heads the list of signatories of the Proclamation. He was executed on 3 May 1916.

MICHAEL COLLINS (1890–1922) Michael Collins was born in County Cork. He worked as a clerk in London, where he joined the IRB and the GAA. He returned to Ireland in 1915 and was close to the men of the 'Kimmage Garrison' (see JOSEPH PLUNKETT below) and the Plunkett family. He fought in the GPO and was interned after the defeat of the insurgents. He took a prominent part in the War of Independence and supported the Treaty. He was killed in action in the Civil War on 22 August 1922.

JAMES CONNOLLY (1868–1916) James Connolly was born in Edinburgh to Irish parents. From an early age, he was obliged to work. At the age of fourteen, he joined the British army; he was stationed in Cork for the next seven years. In 1889, he founded the Irish Republican Party, and the Workers' Republic. After going on a lecture tour in America, he accepted a job in Belfast organising the ITGWU, Jim Larkin's newly founded union. Connolly was involved in the 1913 Lockout, and he was instrumental in founding the Irish Citizen Army. With the outbreak of war in 1914, he determined to lead the labour movement in a fight for Ireland's independence. He was brought into secret talks with the IRB. He decided to join forces with the IRB and was co-opted onto its Military Council. Connolly was a signatory of the Proclamation. He was Commander General of the Dublin Division during the Rising and was stationed at the GPO. He was executed at Kilmainham Jail on 12 May 1916.

ÉAMON DE VALERA (1882–1975) Éamon de Valera was born in New York. At the age of two, he was sent to live with his grandmother in County Limerick. He graduated in mathematics from the Royal University in 1904. He joined the Gaelic League in 1908 and the Irish Volunteers in 1913. In 1916, de Valera commanded the garrison at Bolands Mills. He later took a significant part in the Irish independence movement. He was president of Sinn Féin from 1917 to 1926 and was made President of the First Dáil in 1919 and President of the Irish Republic in 1921. He opposed the Treaty and resigned when the Dáil ratified it. In 1927, he established the Fianna Fáil party and in 1932 led the party into government. In 1932, the Fianna Fáil government put the Constitution, largely the work of de Valera, to a referendum. He was Taoiseach and Minister for External Affairs from 1937 to 1948 and again from 1951 to 1954 and from 1957 to 1959. He was President from 1959 to 1973. His political aim remained a thirty-two-county Gaelic republic.

ARTHUR GRIFFITH (1871–1922) Arthur Griffith was born in Dublin in 1871. He was apprenticed as a printer. From 1893 to 1910, he was active in the Gaelic League and the IRB. In South Africa, he fought for the Boers. In 1904, he wrote *The Resurrection of Hungary: A Parallel for Ireland,* which promoted economic self-sufficiency and self-government for Ireland. In 1906, he founded Sinn Féin. He joined the Irish Volunteers in 1913 but took no part in the 1916 Rising. He was imprisoned and released in 1917. He led the Irish delegates in the Treaty negotiations in late 1921. In 1922, he died from a cerebral haemorrhage.

JAMES LARKIN (1876–1947) James Larkin was born in Liverpool in 1876. His parents were Irish and he was reared in County Down. On returning to :Liverpool, he worked on the docks and became involved in the trade-union movement. He organised the dock labourers in Liverpool, Belfast and Dublin. In 1908, he founded the ITGWU. In 1911, he became president of the Irish Congress of Trades Unions. He led the workers in the 1913 Lockout and was imprisoned from 1913 to 1914. On his release, he left for America, where he continued his work as a trade unionist. He was imprisoned again in 1920. He returned to Ireland in 1923 and was expelled from the ITGWU, probably for ideological reasons. He founded the Irish Workers' Union in 1923. He was elected to the Dáil in 1926 and held his seat intermittently until 1944. He died in 1947.

DR KATHLEEN LYNN (1874–1955) Kathleen Lynn was born in County Mayo, the daughter of a Church of Ireland rector and a relative of Countess Markievicz. She qualified as a doctor in 1899 and in 1904 set up in practice in Rathmines. In 1913 she became a supporter of the labour movement. She subsequently joined the Irish Citizen Army and took part in the 1916 Rising, serving in the garrison at City Hall. After the Rising, she was imprisoned and forced into exile in England. When she returned to Ireland, no hospital would employ her. She practised as a doctor during the War of Independence and in 1919 established the first infant hospital in Ireland.

SEAN MCDERMOTT (1884–1916) Sean McDermott was born in County Leitrim. In his youth he worked as a tram conductor in Belfast – where he was sworn into the IRB. In 1908, he was transferred to Dublin, where he became a close friend of Thomas Clarke. From this time on, he devoted all his time to the Brotherhood, travelling throughout Ireland organising the movement. He became its best-known and most popular leader. In 1913, he was one of the founding members of the Irish Volunteers. McDermott was secretary of the Supreme Council and the Military

Council of the IRB. He was a signatory of the Proclamation and a member of the Provisional Government. He was executed on 12 May 1916.

THOMAS MACDONAGH (1878–1916) Thomas MacDonagh was born in Cloughjordan, County Tipperary, and educated at Rockwell College and University College Dublin. He joined the Gaelic League in 1901 and helped Patrick Pearse found St Enda's School in Ranelagh, Dublin, in 1908. In 1911, he became a university lecturer, and he co-founded the *Irish Review*. He was a founder member of the Irish Volunteers in 1913 and became a member of the IRB in 1915. He was co-opted onto the Military Council of the IRB only a few weeks before the Rising. He was a signatory of the Proclamation and was execured on 3 May 1916.

EOIN MACNEILL (1867–1945) Eoin MacNeill was born in County Antrim. He was the first vice-president of the Gaelic League and the first professor of early and medieval Irish history at University College Dublin. He was the founder of the *Feis Ceoil* and was Chief of Staff of the Irish Volunteers. In 1916, he countermanded the orders of the IRB Military Council for manoeuvres on Easter Sunday when he found out that they were a cover for the Rising – with which he disagreed. He later supported the Treaty.

COUNTESS MARKIEVICZ (1868–1927) Constance Gore-Booth (Countess Markievicz) was a member of the Anglo-Irish Gore-Booth family of Lissadell, County Sligo. In her late twenties she became interested in nationalism and social issues, and she joined Inghinidhe ne hÉireann. She later joined Cumann na mBan and was a founder member of the Fianna. During the 1913 Lockout, she served in the soup kitchens in support of the workers. She joined the Citizen Army and fought in the Rising. She was sentenced to death for her part in the Rising but the sentence was commuted to life imprisonment. In 1918, she was elected to the House of Commons but did not take her seat. Countess Markievicz opposed the Treaty. She joined the Fianna Fáil Party in 1926. She was elected to the Dáil in 1927 but died later that year.

HELENA MOLONY (1884–1967) At nineteen years of age, Helena Molony joined Inghinidhe na hÉireann. In 1909, she helped found the Fianna. She subsequently became an actress in the Abbey Theatre. In 1913, Molony joined the labour movement. She did secretarial work for James Connolly and became a member of the Irish Citizen Army. In the 1916 Rising, she was part of the garrison at City Hall; afterwards, she was imprisoned in both Irish and English jails. In the ensuing War of Independence, Molony acted as a courier for Michael Collins and Liam Mellows. In the 1930s and

1940s, she continued to be active on behalf of women workers. She became a member of Mna na hÉireann, seeking equal rights and opportunities for women.

PATRICK PEARSE (1879–1916) Patrick Pearse's father was from England and his mother was from County Meath. He was educated at the Christian Brothers School at Westland Row in Dublin and at the Royal University. He was called to the Bar but did not practise. His interest in the Irish language led him to join the Gaelic League, and he became editor of its newspaper, *An Claideamh Soluis*. Pearse at first supported Home Rule but later became convinced that physical force was necessary if independence was to be achieved. Pearse was recruited into the IRB in 1912 and later became a member of its Military Council. He was head of the Provisional Government of the Irish Republic and delivered the Proclamation of Independence on Easter Monday 1916. On 29 April, Pearse surrendered, and he was executed on 3 May 1916.

JOSEPH MARY PLUNKETT (1887–1916) Joseph Plunkett was born in Dublin, the son of George Noble, Count Plunkett. Joseph Plunkett had close ties with literary Dublin and was editor of the *Irish Review*. He joined the IRB and the Irish Volunteers. He helped Roger Casement in his efforts to secure German help for the Rising. The Plunkett estate in Kimmage was used as a training camp for the returned emigrants who were to take part in the Rising; it was known as the Kimmage Garrison. Plunkett was a member of the Military Council of the IRB and was a signatory of the Proclamation. He married Grace Gifford in Kilmainham Jail on the eve of his execution, 4 May 1916.

JOHN REDMOND (1856–1918) John Redmond was born in County Wexford. He was elected an MP in 1881. He became leader of the Irish Parliamentary Party after the death of Parnell, of whom he was an ardent supporter. He was responsible for the introduction of the 1912 Home Rule Bill and believed that Ireland's support for the war in 1914 would secure Home Rule.

CHRONOLOGY

1914: 4 August

War declared. Home Rule for Ireland shelved for the duration of the War. *20 September* John Redmond, leader of the Irish Parliamentary Party, urges the Irish Volunteers to enlist in the British army. This causes a split in the Volunteers: 170,000 leave the organisation and follow John Redmond, forming the National Volunteers. Only 11,000 remain in the Irish Volunteers under Eoin MacNeill. Many of Redmond's followers enlist in the British army, joining those Irish already serving there. The bulk of Irish recruits come from among the urban working class. For the next four years, the war between the two great imperial powers Britain and Germany rages, mainly on the continent of Europe. Thousands of Irishmen fight in the war.

1915: May

The IRB Executive appoints a Military Council to make detailed plans for the Rising. The Council appoints Patrick Pearse, Joseph Plunkett and Éamonn Ceannt as leaders of the Rising. These men liaise with Tom Clarke and Sean McDermott, long-time members of the IRB who are fully committed to the need for a Rising.

1916: January

James Connolly is persuaded to join forces with this inner group. He is voted on to the Military Council, ensuring that the Citizen Army will be involved in the Rising. Thomas MacDonagh is elected to the Council a few weeks before the Rising.

Sunday 9 April

Following intensive representations in Germany by Sir Roger Casement, the *Aud* (formerly the *Libeau*) sets out from Germany carrying 20,000 rifles. Three days later, Casement boards a German submarine for a planned rendezvous with the *Aud* in Kerry.

19

Wednesday 19 April

The *Aud* arrives in Tralee Bay. It is unable to land the arms because there is no signal from the shore.

Friday 21 April

Casement, along with Robert Monteith and David Bailey, go ashore. Casement is captured a few hours later. The *Aud* is taken by the British navy.

Saturday 22 April

The Captain of the *Aud* scuttles the ship and the arms are lost. Eoin MacNeill, Chief of Staff of the Irish Volunteers, issues an order countermanding the order for manoeuvres to be held on Sunday 23 April – a cover for the Rising, which was planned for that day. Couriers are sent out all over the country with the new order. MacNeill also has a notice of the cancellation of manoeuvres published in the *Sunday Independent*.

Sunday 23 April

The Military Council meets in Liberty Hall to discuss the situation and to revise its plans. The Rising is postponed until Monday 24 April. Patrick Pearse is elected President and Commander General of the Irish Republic. James Connolly is to be Vice-President and Commander-General of the Dublin Division, thus fusing the two wings of the republican army.

Monday 24 April

Almost 1,600 insurgents assemble at various locations for the Rising. The small number is the result of the confusion caused by the sudden changes in instructions and the secrecy imposed by the Military Council. At noon, the Rising begins, with the occupation of the GPO, which had been chosen as the headquarters for the insurrection. Pearse is joined by James Connolly, Tom Clarke, Sean McDermott and Joseph Plunkett. Other key buildings in central Dublin are taken and held by the insurgents. These include, on the north side of the city, the Four Courts, under the command of Ned Daly, and on the south side the Mendicity Institute, with Sean Heuston in command., and the South Dublin Union, under the command of Éamonn Ceannt. Thomas MacDonagh heads the garrison at the Jacob's factory (now the National Archives). St Stephen's Green and, later, the College of Surgeons are occupied by a section of the Citizen Army under Commandant Michael Mallin and Countess Markievicz. The men at Bolands Mills fight under Éamon de Valera. From these bases, the insurgents fan out in an effort to hold the British and prevent the recapture of strategic buildings for as long as possible. The Proclamation of the creation of the Irish Republic is posted up outside the GPO. By afternoon, the insurgents hold most of the city centre. A small contingent of the Citizen Army attacks Dublin Castle: a policeman is killed; the attackers fail to take Dublin Castle. They withdrew to City Hall, where their leader, Sean Connolly, is shot by a sniper in the Castle. Sean Heuston begins his long defence of the Mendicity Institute, with just twenty men. The Lancers try to retake the GPO. As they withdraw, they leave the dead horse which makes such an impression on some of the witnesses.

Tuesday 25 April

Before daylight, the British have machine-guns at the Shelbourne Hotel, the United Services Club and Trinity College, and field guns are on their way from Athlone. Early in the morning, the Irish positions come under sustained fire. More Volunteers, from Kildare and other places, begin to arrive at the GPO. A small detachment of these, with some of the Hibernian Rifles, are sent to fend off the British, who have by this time retaken City Hall. A thousand British troops arrive from the Curragh at 3.45 PM. Others come from Belfast. By the end of the day, 6,627 British officers and men are in Dublin. The St Stephen's Green Garrison withdraws to the College of Surgeons. The Broadstone Railway Station is recaptured by the British. That evening, martial law is declared.

Wednesday 26 April

The shelling of Liberty Hall begins in the morning. (The building had been abandoned by the Citizen Army and was empty.) Later, the gunboat *Helga* joins in the bombardment. At about 9 AM, Lieutenant Malone of de Valera's battalion receives a despatch telling him that more than 2,000 British reinforcements are advancing towards his position at Mount Street from Kingstown (now Dun Laoghaire). He is to hold them off for as long as possible. The ensuing engagement lasts all day. Malone and his band of nine men hold up the advance of two full British battalions, inflicting 234 casualties. At the end of the engagement, Malone is killed by a hail of bullets in a house which he had himself defended for five hours with the aid of just one companion. Incendiary shells start fires in Sackville Street (now O'Connell Street). The fires rage through large parts of Dublin for the next four days. In London, the government decides to send over General Maxwell to quash what remains of the Rising.

Thursday 27 April

At the GPO, James Connolly is wounded twice, once in the arm and once by a ricocheting bullet in the ankle. The British hold the city in a firm grip. The struggle to hold the South Dublin Union, which has been going on for four days, continues. The British make one more attack, at 3 PM. The fighting lasts for the next six hours. Cathal Brugha, who has held the British back for more than two hours, is wounded more than twenty-five times. All the buildings around the GPO are in flames. Ned Daly's positions round the Four Courts are attacked. It takes the North and South Staffordshire Regiments two days to capture North King Street, with fighting going house by house and yard by yard. They lose five officers and forty-two men. Later that evening, members of the 2nd Battalion South Staffordshires run amok: in all, fifteen men and boys who had no connection with the Rising are killed in North King Street.

Friday 28 April

By 6 PM, it is clear that the garrison at the GPO will have to either break out or surrender. At 8 PM, they decide to break out, hoping to link up with the garrison at the Four Courts. The O'Rahilly is killed in the attempt. Eventually, the main body of Volunteers gets into some houses in Moore Street and tunnels its way through to O'Hanlon's Fish Market. On Friday too, the Battle of Ashbourne takes place. Thomas Ashe and his second-in-command, Richard Mulcahy, take more than ninety prisoners, capture four police barracks and decisively defeat a detachment of RIC.

Saturday 29 April

At noon, Pearse and his colleagues decide to surrender. Elizabeth O'Farrell, one of the few members of Cumann na mBan to have stayed with the Volunteer garrison in its dash from the GPO to Moore Street, carries the white flag of surrender towards the British barricade. Brigadier Lowe, the Commander of the British Forces in Ireland, insists on unconditional surrender, to which the Volunteers agree. Before marching out from 16 Moore Street, the garrison kneels and says the Rosary. James Connolly, who has been brought to the military hospital at Dublin Castle, also agrees to unconditional surrender for the men under his command.

Sunday 30 April

All Saturday afternoon and most of Sunday, Elizabeth O'Farrell goes to the various Irish commands, carrying the order to surrender. She is accompanied by Captain de Courcey Wheeler, aide-de-camp to Brigadier Lowe.

FOREWORD

On 11 March 2003, the Bureau of Military History was formally opened to the public. Situated in the Military Archives at Cathal Brugha Barracks in Rathmines, Dublin, the Bureau was established in January 1947 after protracted discussions lasting well over a decade. Its stated aim was 'to assemble and co-ordinate material to form the basis for the compilation of the history of the movement for independence from the formation of the Irish Volunteers on 25 November 1913 to 11 July 1921.' The bulk of the documents that comprise the Bureau of Military History consists of statements tendered to the appointed members of the Bureau by witnesses of the events between those two dates – in all, 1,770 statements.

When the Bureau members had completed their task, they oversaw the placing of the witness statements into 83 steel boxes, together with 66 annexes to witness statements, 54 collections of records of people who did not contribute statements, 178 collections of press cuttings, 12 voice recordings, 246 photographs and 322 bundles of original documents. In March 1959, this major archive was locked in the strongroom in Government Buildings, not to be released to researchers and the general public until after the death of the last recipient of the military-service pension who had testified to the Bureau.

On that spring evening in March 2003, there was a buzz of excited chatter in the hall in Cathal Brugha Barracks; the buzz died down as An Taoiseach Bertie Ahern TD and Minister for Defence Michael Smith TD took their places on the platform. A former Taoiseach, Liam Cosgrave, whose father, William T. Cosgrave, had led the first Free State government, was also present, as were numerous children and grandchildren of witnesses. Chief of Staff Lieutenant General C. Mangan, uniformed officers and soldiers of the Irish army were in attendance. Elderly historians, hardly believing that they finally would have access to the contents of the Bureau archive, had an air of contented expectancy. Almost forty years previously, on the occasion of the fiftieth anniversary of the 1916 Rising, Professor F. X. Martin had glumly described the inaccessible Bureau of Military History as being cut off from the public by an 'official iron curtain'. Present also were young historians, aware that their generation would benefit from the opening of the archives. Diarmaid Ferriter, whose comprehensive history of Ireland, *The Transformation of Ireland, 1900–2000,* was published in 2004, drew on material from the records, and in an essay he wrote for *Dublin Review 12* on the Bureau of Military History he stated: 'The definitive history of the 1916 Rising has yet to be written; these statements will be indispensable for those who seek to write it.'

Annie Ryan is the first writer to exploit the full range of witness material in the Bureau of Military History that deals with the 1916 Rising. Daughter of Tom Harris, a former TD for Kildare, she was well placed to take on the daunting challenge of revealing the scope and complexity of the revolutionary experience. Her father, a Volunteer, was caught up in the Easter Rising in Dublin. On Spy Wednesday, he was summoned from his home in Prosperous, County Kildare, to Newbridge by his area leader, Tom Byrne, who informed him that the Rising would take place shortly. Still awaiting orders on Easter Sunday, Harris's superior officer in the Volunteers, Lieutenant O'Kelly, contacted him about Eoin MacNeill's countermanding order, which had been published that morning in the *Sunday Independent.* Later that afternoon, Patrick Pearse's dispatch, announcing that the Rising was to start at noon on Easter Monday, arrived. After considerable confusion, Harris, O'Kelly and Byrne joined the Maynooth Volunteers and set out on foot for Dublin. What happened subsequently to the Kildare men is threaded throughout Ryan's narrative. For Tom Harris, the events of Easter Week and the time he spent in the General Post Office were 'like one long day':

> I have no recollection of sleeping. On the first night I was at one of the windows, for another period I was on the roof. I remember being in the Instrument Room where it

was first noticed that the Post Office was on fire. The ceilings were arched. You could hear the guns going and I saw a little hole, just a circle, which came in the plaster, about the circumference of a teacup, and I could see this growing. It was evidently caused by an incendiary bomb.

Ryan's narrative is packed with such anecdotes and provides a memorable portrait of the events of Easter Week in Dublin. She identifies minor figures and obscure military encounters such as the fierce fighting around Marrowbone Lane Distillery. The failed attempt on Dublin Castle figures in several witness statements. Depending on where the witness was situated or on duty as a Volunteer, descriptions of the fighting in various parts of O'Connell Street, around City Hall and along the quays provide a different configuration of Dublin city than the one with which we are familiar. Chapter 12, which deals with what took place in the General Post Office, gives startling and revealing vignettes of the chief actors in the drama. According to Min Ryan:

The headquarters people were not doing any fighting in the GPO. They were watching things. Pearse spent most of his time in the front part of the Post Office on one of the high stools, and people would come and talk to him.

Louise Gavan Duffy journeyed by foot from Haddington Road early on Easter Monday morning to the General Post Office in order to reproach Pearse and let him know that she considered the Rising 'a frightful mistake'. She spent the week in the kitchen buttering bread and washing up. Min Ryan remembered 'carving, carving. Very likely, girls came and took the meat around to the men [who] remained at their different posts.' Seamus Robinson recalled that the houses opposite the GPO were on fire and that one building caved in: 'It was at this time that I remember the first shells hitting the roof of the GPO.' Thomas Leahy gave a graphic account of the last few hours of the fighting in the GPO and how the wounded James Connolly 'had to be carried across the bullet-swept street together with the other wounded.'

Despite the passage of years that elapsed between the action of

Easter Week and the taking of the witness statements, there is a remarkable consistency about the accounts, some delivered in a matter-of-fact, impersonal style, others harrowing in their detail. The female relatives of the executed recalled the pathos of the farewells in the hours before the executions. Aine Ceannt, in a rare intimate vignette of her husband Éamonn, said goodbye to him in Irish on Easter Monday, and he enjoined their young son, Ronan, to take care of his mother: *'Aire mhaith dod mhaithrin.'* Aine recounts the reply: '"Tiubhrad, a Dhaide," said Ronan, and so they parted forever.' Nora Connolly O'Brien's recollection of going in an ambulance with her mother to visit her husband James, who lay wounded in bed, and was destined to be shot next morning, is a familiar text of grief borne with dignity which never fails to move the listener. Maurice Collins remembered that he and Sean McDermott were standing side by side in the barrack square in Richmond Barracks awaiting the order for deportation. Said Collins: 'It looks, Sean, as if we will be all together wherever we are going next time.' McDermott replied: 'No, Maurice, the next place you and I will meet will be in heaven.'

Ryan's use of the witness statements opens up fresh considerations about an insurrection about which we think we know everything, because hitherto the selectivity of sources and the successful efforts to mythologise the 1916 Rising, specifically the drama in the GPO, have allowed romantic legends about it to grow. It was less painful for survivors to convert the unbearable into the sentimental, to soften the grim realities that confronted the men and women before they grew silent. Ryan's narrative assembles the events of Easter Week 1916 as experienced by participants whose interlocking stories record in plain language what they saw and endured. Use of the contents of the Bureau of Military History will henceforth alter the manner in which historians treat the personalities and episodes of that period and will also reshape their thinking, and ours, about the generation which was drawn into the revolution and created a new Ireland.

As if anticipating the scepticism of some of her readers, Ryan writes in her introduction: 'The statements are subjective, and we cannot be sure that they conform exactly to the motives and opinions which the interviewees held in 1916. In addition, the people who contributed wanted to do so; there were many who did not.'

Ryan raises a serious issue here. Remembering an experience of such emotional intensity as being an actor in the events of Easter Week in Dublin in the glorious spring weather of April 1916 (several of the statements comment on fine weather) is carried for a lifetime within the living memory of the testament-giver, and fuses with his or her present recall of those hours, days and nights. To the extent that the memories buttress subsequent aspirations and convictions, they have the capacity to be 'co-opted' by different causes.

This issue lies at the core of the revisionist debate in the years following the 1966 commemoration of the Easter Rising: the morality of armed insurrection. The academic jousting that the 'revisionist debate' on the legitimacy of the 1916 Rebellion generated in the 1970s failed, however, to capture the complexity – political, moral, communal – of the parties that were drawn into its vortex. Time never simplifies; it complicates our backward look, and perhaps even unravels the received version of the past. Ryan proffers one reason for treating the statements respectfully. She reflects: 'But if one wishes to "meet" these people and share the emotions and experiences of that extraordinary week and the events that led up to it, the witness statements preserved by the Bureau of Military History cannot be bettered.'

Future historians of the revolutionary period will ignore the archives of the Bureau at the peril of their reputations. A generation which had the capacity to imagine into being an Ireland of citizens and to begin the task of dismantling a colonial way of governing entrusted their written thoughts and feelings on what they had done to a repository that kept them under lock and key for many years. When the statements were eventually opened to the public, did they come too late? Like Derek Mahon's mushrooms in his poem 'A Disused Shed in Co. Wexford', they were waiting for deliverance:

They have been waiting for us in a foetor
Of vegetable sweat since civil war days . . .

A half century, without visitors, in the dark –
Poor preparation for the cracking lock
And creak of hinges.

Ryan's use of the 1916 Rising witness statements is the first study to reveal the rich variety of an unique collection. The photographs that accompany her text document the period and the personalities in a truly authentic fashion. Her book demonstrates that Easter Week 1916 does not belong to any one group exclusively – the Volunteers, the IRB, Cumann na mBan, Sinn Féin, the RIC or British public opinion – but defies co-option. It was the prologue to the Irish revolution.

Margaret Mac Curtain
January 2005

NOTE: Duplicates of the witness statements are available in the National Archives in Bishop Street, Dublin.

INTRODUCTION

The Bureau of Military History took the statements, round which this book is woven, in the years between 1947 and 1957, more than thirty years after the events so vividly described. They were contributed by men and women who had been involved in the movement for independence. One by one, each survivor who agreed to give witness told his or her story. The Bureau appointed senior army personnel and civilians for the task of assembling the material.

Each investigating officer was given intensive training in interview skills and provided with a code of instruction and a chronology of events of the period in order to assist them in obtaining a thorough and accurate account of the witnesses' experience. The statements are subjective, and we cannot be sure that they conform exactly to the motives and opinions which the interviewees held in 1916. In addition, the people who contributed wanted to do so; there were many who did not. But if one wishes to 'meet' these people and share the emotions and experiences of that extraordinary week and the events that led up to it, the witness statements preserved by the Bureau of Military History cannot be bettered.

Although the statements were not contemporary documents, the people who made them were a lot closer to 1916 than we, today, are to the Ireland of 1947 to 1957. Dublin of the 1940s and 1950s for the most part looked very like it did in 1916. The streets and the places that our witnesses frequented – Grafton Street and Dawson Street, Rathmines, Ranelagh and Rathgar, Bride Street and Inchicore – were much the same. The Red Bank restaurant and the Bailey pub were still patronised by people who often met the same people every day.

The strong fabric of society, based as it was on the interlinking friendships of large families, is much in evidence in the witness statements. The camaraderie and ease of social contact between the sexes were stronger in the 1916 period than they are today. Moreover, Irish families were still large in the decade during which the Bureau recorded the statements.

Some of the more interesting witness statements deal with practical matters such as the necessity of feeding large numbers of men when they were engaged in matters of high endeavour. On these occasions, large amounts of meat were required. The women set about providing this, as many of them would have done at the threshings which, in the 1940s, were still common at harvest time in rural Ireland. One is lost in admiration for the stamina of these young women – not to mention the fact that so many of them could carve! Moreover, the use of terms like 'servant boy' and 'master's man' remind us of how many years have passed since those terms became unacceptable.

The great majority of the statements are narrative in style, but even within these limits, they are extraordinarily varied. Some witnesses are self-consciously reticent, for example saying 'we' when they clearly mean 'I'; others warm to their subject, becoming quite flowery in their language. The spare, laconic style of many of the female witnesses, when describing intensely emotional events, was typical of the Anglo-Irish Edwardians still surviving in the 1940s.

By the time these statements were written, some of the witnesses would have you believe that they were now signed-up pacifists. Maybe they were: much had happened in the years since 1916. For the most part, they had reached late middle age, but the record of their activity in 1916 shows little evidence of any conscientious objection to the use of physical force.

One of the more intriguing themes that impinge from a reading of the statements is the importance of the Irish Republican Brotherhood before the Rising, not only in Ireland, but also in the countries where thousands of Irish emigrants sought a livelihood. The IRB was a secret revolutionary organisation founded in 1856. It was dedicated to the establishment of a free republic in Ireland, by physical force if necessary. In the late nineteenth.century, its fortunes were to a large extent eclipsed by the Home Rule movement, which aimed to achieve a form of independence by constitutional means. A change in public attitudes towards the means by which independence should be achieved was discernible in the early part of the twentieth century, and the IRB took full advantage of this shift. Not surprisingly, the seven signatories of the 1916 Proclamation were members of the IRB. But others too were members of the IRB long before the Rising. One unlikely member was Tim Healy, who was a barrister, an MP at Westminster and the first Governor-General of the Irish State. Another was James O'Connor, the head of the nationally known O'Meara's bacon firm. On the other hand, William T. Cosgrave and Éamon de Valera, both of whom took part in the Rising, were never members of the IRB.

During the 1940s and 1950s, the IRB was hardly mentioned publicly, and yet the witness statements are full of references to the organisation. We find accounts of the old tradition passed down from father to son (never to daughters). Occasionally, whole families of sons were members. Sometimes the young men resigned from the organisation on getting married, but they never forgot the Brotherhood and were always ready to help out if asked, according to some accounts. These men were to be found at times in the most unlikely places, such as for example the Dominican priest Father McClucksey, in Newbridge College, as described by Tom Harris in his witness statement.

As is generally known, the Catholic Church proscribed the IRB, and there are a couple of interesting accounts in the statements of how one got around this situation. As a Protestant, Ernest Blythe, also an IRB man, was intrigued by some of the methods used to salve the consciences of troubled members. Most of the members of the IRB were believing Catholics who said their prayers regularly, and the great majority of these simply believed that the priests were wrong. Yet Denis McCullough, who had almost single-handedly rebuilt the IRB in his native Belfast, refused to allow his men to board the train to Dungannon for the 1916 mobilisation unless they could get a priest to accompany them. The least he could do for his men was to have a priest on hand to administer the last sacraments if they were in danger of death.

Emigration was a fact of life before 1916 and for long afterwards. The importance of the IRB to lonely young men who were living in strange lands and trying to survive – both emotionally and otherwise – is often overlooked. One did not join the IRB, one was invited into the brotherhood. Such an invitation could be quite a boost, particularly for the more serious person. Communication between emigrants and their families at home was not easy. Young emigrants not only missed their families but also almost always lost the companionship of the friends with whom they grew up. In the 1940s and 1950s, this was still a common experience.

Irritations like the presence of a large occupying army in the second-largest city of the British Empire would not of themselves have caused a rebellion, but nonetheless they did not make for a happy populace. The people of Dublin who were old enough to remember the years before 1916 recalled the extraordinary visibility of the British army in Dublin. The soldiers were armed and in uniform and were considered to be a danger to young women. They were confined to the GPO side of O'Connell Street (then Sackville Street). No respectable person would walk on that side of the street after twilight. In peacetime, large garrisons of soldiers were not welcome, even in England. It is significant that those witnesses who reacted most strongly to the presence of soldiers on the streets of Dublin were the female officers of the Citizen Amy. Many of these were also members of Inghinidhe na hÉireann, 'pledged to fight for the complete separation of Ireland from England, and the re-establishment of her ancient culture.' The chief means used by them to achieve this aim was the formation of evening classes for children, where they taught the Irish language and Irish history. They held their classes in the poorer parts of the city, where the British army did much of its recruiting. Right up to the First World War, Inghinidhe na hÉireann issued thousands of leaflets 'addressed to Irish girls telling them not to consort with the enemies of their country.'

Several of the participants in the Rising were good shots. Apart from practising to fight in a rebellion, they had gained their skill as marksmen in shooting as a sport – a popular rural pastime of the Edwardian period – and guns were on open sale in many shops.

The one overriding difference between our own times and those of the Ireland which the witnesses and their contemporaries experienced was the pervading presence of the British Empire. The First World War, which was raging on the battlefields of the Continent while the Irish prepared for rebellion, was an imperial war in that its roots lay in the rivalry between Germany and Britain over colonial trade. In 1914, many Irish people had to face the question of where their primary loyalty lay. Before the war, with the prospect of Home Rule, it was just possible to have it both ways, but not afterwards. The Rising happened when it did because both the Citizen Army and the IRB felt that it must take place before the war ended. The leaders of these organisations wished to exploit the fact that the war distracted Britain from its Irish colony. They also wanted to secure German help in securing Irish independence. Finally, they were keenly aware that the 'Irish question' must not be overlooked in any peace settlement. Theirs was a desperate decision: it was a case of then or never.

The period covered by the witness statements in some cases extends beyond the Easter Week Rising. The story I have attempted to tell through the testimony of the people who lived at the time ends, approximately, with the release of the prisoners at Christmas 1916. Some of the witness statements in this book are not narrative. These non-narrative statements, the most important of which is the famous Castle Document, are discussed in the final chapter. They have a special interest because they deal with matters which were controversial at the time and have been even more so for the historians who drew on them afterwards.

1

'THE WRONG HIP'

On Monday 24 April 1916, the day the Easter Rising began, a young Trinity College graduate left the house of a friend who lived near South Circular Road. All day long, he and his friend had listened to the battle raging outside. There was fighting at the Castle as well as in O'Connell Street. At Kelly's Corner, the Volunteers were defending Davy's public house against the British troops in Portobello. The young graduate was Charles Wyse-Power, a barrister and later a judge. More than thirty years later, he wrote:

> On that evening – Monday – my friend and myself walked down O'Connell Street as far as the GPO to see what was happening. We stood on the pavement opposite the building and I shall not forget the strange atmosphere of that evening. There were no trams, horses, motorcars or traffic of any kind. There was a hush over the street and the Dublin people were standing looking at the flag and wondering what the whole thing was about. Not a shot was to be heard and the only physical facts of what had happened that day was a dead horse about eighty yards on the north side of the Pillar. This horse had been ridden by one of the Lancers. I was struck by the complete stillness. I saw sixteen to twenty extremely tired men each carrying a rifle and led by Domhnall Ó Buachalla coming down Upper O'Connell Street. They wheeled right at the Pillar and entered the GPO.
>
> We were joined by Sir Simon Maddock, a well-known Freemason and Unionist. I said: 'What do you think of this,

Sam?' He said: 'Charlie, you have caught us on the wrong hip this time.' I said: 'What do you think is going to be the end of it?' He said: 'It is a brave thing to have done, and brave men always win.'

The judge was one of those who agreed to give an account of his personal experience of his 'association with national events 1913–1919'. Charles Wyse-Power was a member of the Volunteers as early as 1913. As a first step in this new role, he had taken part in drilling and other routine exercises. Not very long afterwards, however, 'I was told by Sean McDermott and Tom Clarke that I would be more use to them as a lawyer than as an active volunteer.' Years later, the judge made a good witness, giving testimony that was both detailed and graphic.

It was no easy matter to take part in the Easter Rising of 1916: it took years of preparation. The people who were active were in the main young. Some had close connections with an earlier generation of revolutionaries. Others were simply disenchanted with contemporary politics. Many were attracted by the challenge of learning the Irish language and the culture of the Irish people. Events such as the Great War, the activities of the Ulster Volunteers, and the sheer boredom induced by the slow pace of Home Rule campaigns combined to make the Rising almost inevitable.

That the Rising was mounted at all was extraordinary. As it was, what was meant to take place on Easter Sunday happened on Easter Monday, and what was planned for the whole island became almost completely a Dublin affair. The events of the Rising were to be crammed into one long week – a weekthat would never be forgotten by the survivors who gave their evidence. Each statement is unmistakably individual. The language used – the turn of phrase, the cadences of the sentences – give indications of class and geography. Some of the statements convey an exhilaration that had been keenly felt thirty years before; others are sad, and some are brokenhearted. By the time the Bureau began its work in 1947, witnesses were more than ready to explain why they had been involved in the Rising and what they had done in it. Some people had to go back a good few years to make their position absolutely clear: for instance, by stating that they been members of the IRB long before the Rising.

Doctor Kathleen Lynn, who was born in Mallaghfarry in Mayo, two miles from Killala, was the daughter of a clergyman and a fellow of the Royal College of Surgeons:

It was quite in a casual way I first got in touch with the national movement. Helena Molony was ill and Mme Markievicz came and asked me to go and see her. I did not know Mme Markievicz, although she was a distant cousin of mine through the Wynns, my mother's people. After Miss Molony got better, she came and stayed with me in Belgrave Road, where I have always lived since I left the hospital. We used to have long talks and she converted me to the National movement. She was a very clever and attractive girl with a tremendous power of making friends. That took place about 1912 or 1913.

Miss Min Ryan – later the wife of General Richard Mulcahy – was a member of the remarkable Ryan family from Wexford, who were deeply involved in 'the National movement'. She attributes her family's involvement in this movement to her eldest brother, Martin – later Father Martin Ryan – who was then in Maynooth College as a student:

At that time (1902–06), Maynooth was leader of young opinion, especially regarding the language, and afterwards regarding Sinn Féin. There were a large number of students, particularly the Ferns men, who were interested in these movements. They had a new outlook as to the means of attaining freedom. I remember my brother coming home at holiday time and talking tremendously about the language and Sinn Féin. We started to read papers about every single thing that was said by Arthur Griffith in connection with the Sinn Féin movement. At that time it was only ourselves in our locality had that sort of interest.

Claire Gregan (who later married Bulmer Hobson) took a different route:

> I was working as a typist for Bulmer Hobson for about six months before the Rising. I was doing his private work and was not working for anybody else. It was he brought me in. I am not absolutely certain that I was engaged to him when I took the job but I think I was.

It was his desire to learn the Irish language that brought Ernest Blythe into the movement. Blythe, born the son of a Protestant farmer at Maghergall, near Lisburn, County Antrim, came to Dublin in March 1905 to work as a 'boy clerk' in the Department of Agriculture. He was not yet sixteen:

> I had always wanted to learn Irish . . . Within about an hour of coming to town I heard three people speaking Irish outside the Gaelic League bookshop, which occupied the building where Mackey's seed shop now is. Having stood looking at the books in the window and listening to the Irish-speaking group as long as they talked, I went and bought the first book of O'Growney's Easy Lessons, which I began studying that night in the Queen's Theatre during the intervals of a melodrama called *The Lights of London*, the first play I had ever seen.
>
> For several months I was afraid to join the Gaelic League because I believed that if it were discovered that I was a Protestant I should be put out.

When he learned that Douglas Hyde, also a Protestant, was, to say the least, a prominent member of the Gaelic League, Blythe joined the League. Blythe's first teacher was Sinead Ni Fhlannagain, who later married Éamon de Valera. Blythe continues:

> After I had been four or five months in the Branch, carefully keeping myself to myself, I began to talk to my classmate, George Irvine, and he told me about Griffith's paper, *United Ireland*. . . . I became converted to Sinn Féin on the night I sat up reading my first copy of the *United Irishman*.

His conversion to nationalism progressed to the point where he joined the IRB, recruited by the playwright Sean O'Casey.

Aine Ceannt, widow of Éamonn Ceannt, who was executed for the part he played in the Rising, writes:

> After the Parnell split, there was no interest taken in politics by the young folk. There were too many divisions. The Gaelic League, where there were no politics spoken, was a Mecca for everyone. The people learned that they had a country with a language; they learned the music, the dancing and the games. They were encouraged to use Irish-manufactured goods, and in the competitions at the Oireachtas of the Gaelic League the competitors would not be awarded a prize unless they could guarantee that they were dressed in Irish materials.

Augustine Ingoldsby, who seems to have been extremely active in cultural circles of a nationalist nature in the early part of the century, is particularly outspoken in his comments on Dublin opinion on political matters:

> We must not forget that it was only a very small majority of the Dublin population kept the nationalist spirit alive. On every occasion, such as the King's visit, all the shopkeepers, merchants, officials of the Corporation, etc, were ready to wave the Union Jack. Of course it was in the interest of their pocket that they did this. Anyone who sold a hat or a pair of shoes to the Castle people put up over their doors: 'Hatters to His Excellency the Lord Lieutenant' etc. For that reason great credit is due to Rooney, Griffith and their followers for keeping up their opposition to the shoneenism and Union Jackery of the vast majority of the population. The Bar was particularly rotten in this respect, because any hint of sympathy with nationalism was a certain hindrance to promotion in their profession.

Helena Molony began her long association with the movement in 1903 when she joined Inghinidhe na hÉireann:

In August 1903, on the evening when I went to join the Inghinidhe at their offices in 196 Great Brunswick Street, I found a notice on the door, which read: 'All come up immediately to 26 Coulson Ave. Raid on the house. (Signed) Dudley Digges.' I immediately repired to that address. It is a little house in Rathgar, where Madame Maud Gonne lived at that time. George Russell was her next-door neighbour. When I arrived in this quiet avenue, I saw a double line of police on the path outside and a similar one on the opposite side. The little front lawn was crowded with the Inghinidhe and many young men (who, I think, were spoiling for a fight). There was a large black flag flying from one of the front windows.

It was a stand-off, but Molony managed to gain entrance. She was accepted into the Society after some explanation. The Inghinidhe were somewhat suspicious of a girl who wanted to join in the midst of this excitement, but:

After eleven o'clock that night I walked home on air, really believing that I was a member of the mystical Army of Ireland. I was at once given some work, and plunged into it with the greatest enthusiasm.

A typical pathway towards participation in the movement was through membership of the Gaelic League, which, considering its mainly cultural genesis, might be thought surprising. The experience of Thomas Harris, in Prosperous, County Kildare, was probably repeated in countless small classes throughout the country, but particularly in Dublin and the surrounding counties. Harris writes:

Our Gaelic League organisation was pretty weak at this time, with the result that our Irish teachers did not remain long with us. About 1913 we had an Irish teacher named Sean O'Connor. He was married and had five or six children, and I think he came from Limerick. He took up residence in Celbridge. I don't think O'Connor was a member of the IRB when he came into the county. He began by bringing *Irish Freedom* and other national papers around to his classes. We would read these papers in the classroom and discuss the political situation of the time. In this way we became more absorbed in political discussion than in our pursuit of the language.

This was the first step in a process of 'politicisation'. The odd feature of this process was that the 'politicisation' almost invariably took place through the medium of English. The initial motive may have been to learn the language, but quite soon the earnest young people who took part in these gatherings were talking politics.

Patrick Kearney from Dublin, who was a decade older than Tom Harris, joined what seemed like a precursor of the Gaelic League. Irish was not taught in the schools in 1897, not even by the Christian Brothers, but in that year William Rooney (whose name crops up in other witness statements, notably those of Augustine Ingoldsby) asked the teachers to send their pupils to his classes in Middle Abbey Street to learn Irish. Kearney, who was then aged thirteen, went along with the rest:

> The Celtic Literary Society met in the same premises, so, in addition to the Irish language classes, we were allowed to attend lectures on the various aspects of Irish affairs.
>
> William Rooney, who was most energetic and enthusiastic, created a very favourable impression on us by giving us a great insight to Irish history. He also wrote ballads and songs. Enough credit has not been given to him for his great efforts to revive the national spirit.
>
> The general tone of the lectures was the futility of the policy of the Irish Parliamentary Party. Among those we met there were Arthur Griffith, Sean T. O'Kelly and Major McBride.

In 1900, the Celtic Literary Society had strongly disapproved of the welcome extended by the members of Dublin Corporation to Queen Victoria. As the century progressed, there was hardly a cultural or political event in which Patrick Kearney did not take part. Individuals like him tended to meet the same people over and over again: he met them at the dramatic classes and language classes, and played hurling with them. He was appointed a clerk on the Strike Committee in the 1913 Lockout. He also knew James Connolly and Jim Larkin. When he went to London in 1910, he knew Michael Collins and Judge O'Byrne, who both worked as clerks in the Post Office there. He knew Countess Markievicz to see:

> The Countess was a prominent figure at the Soup Kitchen, dressed in trousers and smoking cigarettes, both of which were regarded as astonishing things for women to do in those days.

In contrast, the evidence of Sean Murphy, resident caretaker of Dublin Castle, gives an indication of the part taken by the IRB in the national resurgence:

> My first introduction to national affairs was the Commemoration of '98, when I was present at the laying of the foundation stone in St Stephen's Green to Wolfe Tone. About 1900 or 1901 I was approached by a brother-in-law of my own, William Brennan (since deceased), to know if I would be willing to become a member of the IRB. He explained its objects to me, and I was a willing applicant for admission.

Murphy's description of the work he was given to do, and the kind of members who ran his 'club', gives us a valuable insight into the importance of the IRB:

> The club to which I was introduced was named the Thomas Clarke Looby '98 Club. The then Centre [the elected officer of the club] was James O'Connor. He was a representative for all Ireland of the O'Meara Bacon Company. The Secretary was John J. O'Brien, an Auditor whom I after-

wards found out was employed in J. J. Reynold's Auditing Establishment in Westmoreland Street. The Treasurer was John Morrissey, a dairy proprietor in Marrowbone Lane. Those were the three officials of the club at that time.

The young Sean Murphy was appointed Centre of this branch of the IRB. His first job was to reorganise the club and to introduce younger men into it, taking advantage of the new interest in national affairs following the 1898 celebrations. As the personnel of the clubs was in the main elderly, he turned instead to the several Irish Ireland Clubs which were operating at the time. They went so far as to open a drill hall in Strand Street under cover of a gymnasium, but had to close it again when it attracted the attention of the Detective Branch of the police.

Although not everyone who took part in the Rising was a member of the IRB, the influence of the IRB was far greater than the size of its membership would suggest. Sean Murphy tells us that:

> Amongst the active clubs in Dublin were the Michael Dwyer Club, the Red Hand, the Oliver Bond, the Napper Tandy Clubs, and the McHale Branch of the Gaelic League, which first started Inghinidhe na hÉireann, who were the forerunners of Cumann na mBan.
>
> The activities of those Dublin clubs extended all over Leinster, Munster, and partly into the West. Open-air concerts, *aeridheacht,* concerts in general, *ceilidhthe,* etc, Irish, Ireland songs, dancing, etc were carried out to revive the spirit of the men of '98 and to bring it forward into our day for our own movement. In this way the GAA and Gaelic League were utilised by our members as the organising ground for our recruiting campaign.

Some witnesses give us little or no clue in their statements as to how they set out on the road which led to the 1916 Rising and beyond. One such was Cornelius 'Con' O'Donovan. O'Donovan was from Cork and a member of the IRB. He was one of the few students, apart from those connected with St Enda's School and Patrick Pearse, who took part in the events of Easter 1916. He does not tell us how or where he joined the IRB. Perhaps he came from an old Fenian family, like the Boland brothers, Gerald, Harry and Edmund – and whose sister Kathleen later married Cornelius's brother Sean.

Few women knew anything about the IRB, at least officially. This did not prevent Mairín Cregan from being thoroughly imbued with enthusiasm for all things Irish:

> As a child in Killorglin, my mother talked a good deal about Douglas Hyde and the language movement. She made her children learn Irish dancing and singing and tried to recall Irish phrases heard from her own parents to teach them to us.

Later, Mairín was sent to boarding school – St Louis Convent in Carrickmacross, County Monaghan – where she met two nieces of Domhnall Ó Buachalla from Kilcock, County Meath, and two nieces of Eoin MacNeill from Glenarm, County Antrim. In those days, children were sent far away for their education, to schools which reflected the values of their parents. They were lucky to find a school which, unlike the great majority of secondary boarding schools at the time, was not 'bereft of all nationality', as Senia Paseta puts it in her book *Before the Revolution*. On the contrary, at St Louis:

> The headmistress, Sister Stanislaus McCarthy, a Cork woman, encouraged us in every way to speak Irish.

Mairín Cregan later married Dr James Ryan from County Wexford, a long-serving minister in the Fianna Fáil government throughout the 1930s, 1940s and 1950s.

2

'Something Serious in the Wind'

There was then in Dublin, particularly amongst the young, a general distaste for what passed as adult politics at the time; it was all regarded as being too smug. It was not that people were ecstatic about British rule or royal visits and the social life and business opportunities associated with the Castle, but there was an air of pragmatism and compromise to be found, especially in the middle classes, which was not attractive, particularly to the young. The efforts of the elite to adopt the ways of the landed gentry or to become as Protestant as they could be without actually attending church was a wearisome burden on that small section of the Catholic Irish who could be described as successful. It is no wonder that so many of the young elite, who were beginning to emerge in the newly established National University of Ireland and its affiliated colleges, turned to something quite different.

Life in Dublin in the years leading up to 1916 must have been very exciting, particularly if one was young and radical. Mairín Cregan, who grew up in Killorglin, County Kerry, got her first job, teaching, in the Brigidine Convent in Goresbridge, County Kilkenny. She was already interested in the language movement, and at least one of the nuns there shared her interests. It was at Goresbridge that Mairín became friends with Margaret Browne, who had a first-class degree in Irish and Celtic studies and came weekly from Dublin to give lectures to the nuns. The two young women became friendly. In September 1914, Cregan came to Dublin to study music. She recalls:

When I got settled into digs in Rathmines, Miss Browne spent all her weekends with me. Later Miss Kay Brady of Belfast, who also taught at St Louis, joined us. Miss Browne introduced me to Miss Kit Ryan (afterwards Mrs Sean T. O'Kelly), who kept open house every Sunday evening for young and old who were Sinn Féiners, Gaelic Leaguers, Volunteers, etc. Here we met people like Sean McDermott, Sean T. O'Kelly, Liam O'Briain (now Professor of Romance languages, Galway University), Father Paddy Browne (now President, Galway University), [and] Padraig O'Conaire. Practically every Saturday night we went to the Abbey Theatre and afterwards to a *ceilidhe*. I was taking singing lessons from Madame Coslett Heller and soon I was requisitioned for singing at Volunteers' concerts. So I might say that my active association with the national movement in Dublin before the Rising was singing at Volunteer concerts.

In his statement, Father Paddy Browne remembered meeting, in addition to the people named by Mairín, Charles Wyse-Power and his sister Nancy, and Senator Michael Hayes. He often met Sean McDermott at the Ryans' place. But the men also spent a considerable amount of their time at the headquarters of the Volunteers in Dawson Street; Cumann na mBan had their office in the same building. Miss Min Ryan, another of the Ryan sisters, worked there as one of the secretaries of Cumann na mBan. Father Browne became very friendly with Sean McDermott in the months before the Rising:

I used to go to his office and I used to meet him in the smoke-room in the Bailey. He would just turn in there like anyone else, just coming for a drink or a smoke. His conversation was of a general nature and had absolutely nothing to do with the Volunteers. . . . At no time did he give me any inkling that there was anything serious in the wind.

Sean T. O'Kelly held his 'open house' on a Wednesday, presumably so that it would not clash with the one on Sunday night over at the Ryans' in Ranelagh.

Ernest Blythe did not socialise in quite the same circles. For one thing, he was not in Dublin in 1913 or 1914. Even when he lived in the city after he had joined the Gaelic League, he was inclined to keep himself to himself. But when he took up hurling, he became friendly with Sean O'Casey:

> After we had known one another for some months, both of us being very bad hurlers and never getting on the team but practising zealously in the Phoenix Park every Saturday and going together to see the matches in which the club team played, Sean began to talk to me about the Fenians.

It turned out that the young Ernest Blythe was being recruited to the IRB by the playwright; he subsequently joined the organisation. He was just eighteen when he joined; his membership certainly broadened his circle of acquaintances in Dublin. When he returned to Belfast at the the age of twenty – he was now too old to continue as a boy clerk in the Department of Agriculture and instead secured a job as a journalist on the *North Down Herald* – his membership of the IRB provided him with ready-made contacts outside those he might meet in relation to his work. He immediately met the members of the Belfast IRB, which had been reorganised by Denis McCullough some years before.

Later in 1913, he carried out his plan of making a concerted effort to learn his beloved language from the people who still spoke it in the course of their daily life. It was only after taking the momentous step of moving to the Dingle peninsula in County Kerry to work as a farm labourer that Blythe really made friends.

Armed with letters of introduction, which he had procured in Killarney from 'The Seabhac', on his way to this strange place where he knew nobody, he proceeded in stages to Dingle. On his very first morning there, he was, as he recalls:

hailed by a man with an English accent who had heard about me from Mrs O'Shea (Eilis de Barra), on whom The Seabhac had advised me to call. The man was Desmond FitzGerald, who had come to live at Ballintaggart, a mile outside Dingle, only three or four days before.

But, most marvellous of coincidences of all, Blythe found that FitzGerald's wife was, like himself, a Northern Protestant:

I found that Mrs Fitzgerald came from Donaghadee, where as a reporter at Petty Sessions, I had often met her father, who was an exceedingly cranky magistrate. I was with the FitzGeralds practically every Sunday during the period I remained in Kerry.

Eventually, Blythe was accepted into the Ashe family to work on the family farm, through the intervention of Sean McDermott, who knew Thomas Ashe, a member of the family in Dublin. Thomas Ashe worked as a teacher and was very likely a member of the IRB. He played a prominent part in the 1916 Rising and was to die on hunger strike during the War of Independence. But that was all in the future. Blythe went on to learn Irish the hard way – which was never to speak a word of English. No matter how much he might want to say something, he would wait until he 'got the Irish' for it.

Generally speaking, the people who gave their testimony – which was sometimes very personal – made the effort to give as clear and dispassionate an account as they could of how they acted, how they felt and what they thought, all those years ago. There are a few, perhaps, whose memories are somewhat too reflective of later debates and later discussions. Josephine MacNeill, in an otherwise enchanting account of her connections and friendships with some of those who were active in the movement, would have us believe that Ginger O'Connell, whom she met for the first time as she came out of lectures at UCD, firmly held that the mystical tendencies of the Executive of the Volunteers should be held in check by Eoin MacNeill:

One day in 1914, coming out of lectures, I remember seeing a man older than ourselves with a wide round hat. It was Ginger O'Connell. I made his acquaintance and on a subsequent occasion he informed me that on the outbreak of war he had deserted from the American army as he felt the time was opportune to return and help to organise resistance against the British in his own land. At this time he was an organiser for the Volunteers and was constantly at No. 2 Dawson Street.

Josephine became very friendly with Ginger during 1914 and 1915. No doubt she met those others who frequented No. 2 Dawson Street. Despite her close connections with people who were heavily involved with the national movement, she had no idea, when she went to Belfast to stay with her friend Mrs Joseph Connolly in early April, that a Rising was imminent. Josephine missed the Rising but she met Ginger again when he was imprisoned with many others in Kilmainham Jail: she was amongst the large crowd of wives and girlfriends who visited the prisoners. It was difficult to make contact with anyone in particular but Josephine managed it:

> After some efforts on my part and the co-operation of a decent English officer, whose name I can't remember, I was allowed to see Ginger O'Connell separately in some sort of barrack room. The officer sat there the whole time. When Ginger had gone, the officer, in showing me out, spoke with the greatest respect of the men of Easter Week. He understood from the quality of the prisoners that they were men of high character and motive and superior education and not the riff-raff they were represented [as] by the English and Irish press.

Such remarks were important to Josephine.

Nora Connolly O'Brien, the eldest daughter of James Connolly, opens her witness statement:

> I had always been associated with my father, James Connolly, from the time I was six or seven years of age. He had taken me on lecture tours with him when I was a small child.

Her political career developed from there. She addressed envelopes for the Labour Party when her father stood for the Corporation election in the early 1900s. In 1902, the family went to America, where her father was organising for the Socialist Labour Party and later the Socialist Party. Soon afterwards, he launched the Irish Socialist Federation and at the same time brought out a paper called the *Harp*. When her father had to leave New York, to go on a lecture tour, Nora was left in charge. She was about sixteen years old.

The Connollys returned to Dublin in 1909. Later, James Connolly went to Belfast to work for the Transport & General Workers' Union, where he had important changes made to the ferocious conditions endured by the dockers there. When the mill girls came to Connolly to have him do the same for them, Nora, encouraged by her father, had to make her first speech.

The Fianna, so closely associated with Countess Markievicz, spread to Belfast, where the only girls' branch in Ireland was formed. Connolly O'Brien became the Chief Officer of this branch. When the members formed a political branch, the boys joined too. Here Connolly O'Brien met 'Cathal O'Shannon, Archie Heron, Davy Boyd, Wardlaw and others.' Dublin republican nationalists, including Patrick Pearse, would come and speak at their meetings. The girls and boys would also come down to Dublin every year for the Convention. Connolly O'Brien recalls:

> A lot would come down to attend the Convention, and later go camping with the boys. The girls were usually under Madame Markievicz' charge, when we came down here.

Her most useful friend in Dublin was Liam Mellows:

> who had a friend in Amiens Street Station. When I came on
> the excursion, he always marched me around to Amiens
> Street to this friend of his, who signed the ticket, so that it
> would not cost me extra to stay longer. That is why I was so
> often down here in Dublin. I saved the money for the fares
> from my wages; and Liam would take me to Amiens Street
> Station; and I would stay for a week or so.

It is perhaps not surpising that Nora was familiar with No. 2
Dawson Street, where the Fianna had an office. She was one of
those who formed Cumann na mBan in Belfast too. One of the
first to join was Una Ryan, a sister of Min Ryan and the wife of
Denis McCullough, who had reformed and revived the IRB in
Belfast. The circle of men and women out of which the independence movement grew was small, tight and like a whirlpool. It went
deep into the consciousness of their own generation and generations to follow.

Dr F. de Burca was one of those well-travelled IRB men whose
connections were more valuable before the Rising than they were
during the Rising itself. He was born in 1876 and was admitted to
the IRB in London in 1893. The first job he was asked to do by the
Brotherhood was to organise the GAA in London. His orders were
to make himself as conspicuous as possible, with a view to attract-
ing recruits. Like so many of the brighter young Irish people, he
worked in the British Civil Service, in the Excise Service. He later
had himself transferred to Belfast. There he met old Fenians like
Robert Johnston, father of Eithne Carberry. Johnston, although by
now more interested in his business projects, could always be relied
on for a subscription when asked. Dr de Burca was subsequently
transferred to Kilkenny, where he met Thomas MacDonagh, who
was teaching there. De Burca admitted MacDonagh into the IRB.
He sent his son to St Enda's – which inculcated values shared by de
Burca and other IRB members – and so met Patrick Pearse.

In 1908, Eamon Bulfin entered St Enda's, the school founded

by Patrick Pearse on Oakley Road in Ranelagh. He was the second pupil to enrol there. St Enda's, which later moved to Rathfarnham, was an important nexus in the years leading up to 1916. It was a very different school from the generality of schools. St Enda's hoped to cater for the young people of the new century and was founded with the express purpose of transforming the education system. (In this, Pearse and Eoin MacNeill were at one – even though they disagreed about the proposed rising.) Pearse believed that the Irish education system was founded on a denial of the Irish nation. People who sent their children to St Enda's were no doubt impressed by the school's educational curriculum, which included ancient Irish myths, the Irish language, and Gaelic games. Domhnall Ó Buachalla's son was at school there, as were Jim Larkin's two sons.

Eamon Bulfin, a member of a distinguished family from Birr, County Offaly, and a man who developed strong Argentinian connections, was sent to St Enda's for his secondary education. He continued to reside at the school after he had entered UCD in 1912 to study science. Bulfin had proposed the admission of Pearse into the IRB, not the other way round:

> This proposal was received with some diffidence, as Pearse had appeared on a Home Rule platform in favour of the Council's Bill.

Bulfin himself was sworn into the IRB standing on top of Wolfe Tone's grave in Bodenstown churchyard. Bulfin was friends with Con Colbert and Liam Mellows, who were well known to new recruits to the Brotherhood throughout the country. They used to drill at 41 Parnell Square – the Foresters' Hall – using dummy rifles and small arms. They were frequently visited by 'Dublin Centres', or leaders, such as Bulmer Hobson, George Irvine and Sean McDermott. Eamon Bulfin told the Bureau:

> When the Volunteers started, most of the older students in St Enda's joined. Most of the older students joined the Rathfarnham Company, especially those who had been sworn into the IRB. I joined the Rathfarnham Company.

Sean T. O'Kelly's experience sheds light on the thoroughness with which the IRB set about harnessing the energy which might flow from organisations and demonstrations, such as the celebrations to mark the centenary of the 1798 Rising. The Parliamentary Party took a prominent part in those celebrations, but they were utilised by a small, effective group who 'had been faithful to the Fenian tradition, and a great number who were still members of the Fenian organisation – the Irish Republican Brotherhood.'

Sean T. O'Kelly himself joined the IRB in 1899. At that time, very few of the older men were still active, but later he met many who were most sympathetic. These older members' connection to an earlier era of the republican movement was valuable to the resurgent movement.

These older IRB members were to be found in the most unexpected places. Judge Charles Wyse-Power in his witness statement describes an encounter with the best-known and perhaps most surprising of these, Tim Healy, an MP, barrister and later Governor-General of the Irish Free State. Wyse-Power enrolled as a Volunteer in 1913, but soon afterwards he was asked by Sean McDermott to cease his Volunteer activities and instead take up his work as a lawyer. He would, McDermott reasoned, be of far more use as a lawyer acting in defence of members of the IRB who were from time to time arrested on charges of sedition. In such cases, Wyse-Power would call on Healy as senior counsel. The latter was almost the only senior counsel who was prepared to defend these cases. Wyse-Power describes one of the meetings held before the trial of Sean Hegarty:

> Before the trial at Green Street we held a couple of conferences to discuss the lines on which the defence was to be conducted, and Sean McDermott was present. Tim Healy did not know who Sean was and he asked about him after the first conference. I told him he was an officer of the organisation to which Hegarty belonged. Tim understood at once that I meant the IRB and he was considerably taken aback. He asked me: 'Do you mean to say that they intend to come out again with the guns?' I said I thought so.

At the next conference, Healy affected not to know anything about Sean McDermott. In the course of the conference, however, McDermott said: 'Mr Healy, do you remember a certain oath you took at Newcastle-on-Tyne on the [no date given] 1879?' mentioning a date on which Tim Healy was enrolled in the IRB in England. From then on, according to Wyse-Power, Healy was always 'at the disposal of the new movement.'

Sean T. O'Kelly was first brought into contact with the IRB via a printer called Patrick Daly. O'Kelly was sworn in by a pharmaceutical chemist called Nally who worked in the Mater Hospital at the time. Almost as soon as he had become a member of the IRB, O'Kelly became a very active recruiter. He recruited many members in Dublin and also in Enniscorthy, Wexford, Arklow, Cork, Galway and Sligo. One Sunday morning 'in 1904 or 1905, in the drawing room of Mrs Barker in South Main Street, I took in ten or twelve new members, among them being Bob Brennan.'

Contrary to claims made by others (in his book *Allegiance*, Brennan maintained that O'Kelly recruited his – Brennan's – wife), O'Kelly denies ever recruiting a woman into the IRB, and he said that, to his knowledge, no woman was ever recruited into the organisation.

The subject of recruitment took up a good deal of time at IRB meetings. Names of prospective members would be put up for discussion and opinions on these people canvassed. O'Kelly recalls that:

> The proposed member would have to be known as a person who was trustworthy, sober, steady and reliable, and our effort was to try to get enlisted well-known men who occupied positions of authority in their own social and business circles.

Members met once a month and paid a subscription of one shilling per month, and another shilling for the arms fund. The IRB monitored the activities of other social, political and national organisations to which their members belonged.

It was an important part of IRB policy that members of the Brotherhood should be actively involved in organisations such as the Gaelic League and the GAA and should make themselves useful to these organisations in any way necessary. This aspect of IRB activity is well known; not so well known, perhaps, is the fact that the IRB was, as Sean T. O' Kelly put it:

> most assiduous in urging support of organisations like the Abbey Theatre, and there would seldom be a night of the Abbey Theatre when many members of the IRB were not present.

Sean McDermott was enlisted into the IRB in Belfast. He was closely associated with Sinn Féin as soon as the organisation was formed and was employed as a full-time organiser for that organisation. He was soon to become a full-time organiser for the IRB, a position he held until the end of his life. In Sean T. O'Kelly's opinion, without Sean McDermott's energy and the encouragement of Tom Clarke, there would have been no Rising in 1916.

In 1915, seven years after McDermott's appointment as an IRB organiser, schoolboys in a Dublin boarding school were busy making munitions, under the direction of IRB man Eamon Bulfin. In his witness statement, Bulfin tells how they made hand grenades which were used during the Rising. Dr Kathleen Lynn, who seems to have been a friend of Pearse's, was called on for help:

> On either Holy Thursday or Good Friday, the munitions were shifted down to Liberty Hall in Dr Kathleen Lynn's motor car. She drove and I was with her. I don't know whether Pearse was actually in St Enda's at the time or not. I think he actually introduced me to Dr Lynn.

The circle was complete.

3

'SOME MEN I COULD TRUST'

Outside Dublin, the importance of the work of organisers for the Volunteers or the IRB (or both) cannot be overlooked. It explains, at least in part, the great swing in sentiment towards separatism and away from a quiescent unionism, which emerged shortly after 1916. Ernest Blythe worked hard for the IRB and wrote extensively of his experiences, first on the Dingle peninsula, and later nearer to his birthplace on the shores of Lough Neagh. His reports and those of the other organisers were an invaluable source of information for the republican leaders in Dublin.

Blythe was sworn into the IRB when he was just eighteen, several years before he took practical steps towards learning Irish from the people who used it in their everyday life. He describes the occasion of his swearing-in:

> After a delay of several months Sean finally told me that I might now be sworn in. . . . I met him in O'Connell Street and was taken to a house on the western side of Parnell Square. A number of people were going up the stairs. I was introduced to Micheal MacAmhlaidh and taken by him into a back room, where he administered the Oath to me. Afterwards I went with Sean into the front room while Micheal MacAmhlaidh was swearing in some other new recruits. The front room was packed. I should say there were over a hundred people in it. When, at one point in the proceedings, new members were asked to stand up and let themselves be seen by the meeting, four or five of us arose.

Recruiting was being pursued very actively at the time. Within a few months, in fact, that particular IRB Circle (or branch), whose cover name was the Bartholomew Teeling Literary and Debating Society, split into three, Blythe reports.

Amongst the members at a meeting of the Circle in a home in Parnell Square, Blythe noticed many who were prominent in other areas of Dublin life. These included Sean T. O'Kelly (later President of Ireland), Cathal Brugha, Louis Carrick, Thomas Cuffe, who was a great friend of Arthur Griffith, and many prominent members of the Gaelic League.

When he was just a month short of twenty years of age, Blythe got a job on the *North Down Herald* in Bangor. He immediately contacted Denis McCullough of the IRB in Belfast, as he had been ordered to do when he left the job. He became a member of the Belfast Circle, which numbered about fifteen members. These included Bulmer Hobson, Sean Lester (later Secretary of the League of Nations), Alf Cotton (who later organised the Volunteers in Kerry) and Cathal O'Shannon. Harry Shiels was also a member: Shiels fought in the Rising in Church Street; he lost an arm after he took a bullet in the elbow. The IRB in Belfast was engaged in a desperate effort to revive the Brotherhood there; Denis McCullough had inherited it in a state of neglect. They were concerned mainly with recruiting, which was a slow business. In Ernest Blythe's opinion:

> Actually circumstances at that time in Belfast were such that it was not possible to do much against the influence of Joe Devlin and the Hibernians on one side and the Orange mob on the other.

In April 1913, Blythe went to live with the Ashe family on their farm in Kerry. On his first visit home, he broke his journey in Dublin, staying over for two weeks or more. While there, he learned the elements of drilling. Soon after his return to Kerry, he was ordered back to Belfast:

> I was written to by Sean McDermott and asked to go up to Belfast to work on an anti-Partition campaign which was to

be started there. Whatever funds were needed were provided by the IRB.

After a couple of months, Blythe was more convinced than ever that they 'could not alter the general complexion of political affairs in Belfast, and that there was nothing more to be done at that juncture.'

He returned to Kerry, where his friend Desmond FitzGerald had had some small success in forming companies of Volunteers. Blythe joined the company at Lispole and took part in the drilling outside the church after Mass. He said that, unfortunately, the skill of the drill instructor left a great deal to be desired. Indeed, the instructor became quite confused on one occasion and gave out the wrong orders to the small group of young men who made up the Company. Their embarrassment was almost too much to bear when the young girls of the parish, who were standing on a bank opposite in order to get a better view of the proceedings, had to hold one another lest they fall, as they shrieked with laughter. Blythe found the laughter of the Kerry girls intolerable:

> I was smitten with a sudden rage, and did what a local man could not have done. I left my place in the ranks, ordered the militia man to step into the vacant space, and proceeded to carry on the drill. From that moment, without further formality, I was Captain of the Lispole Company.

This impromptu promotion was to lead to greater things. He was subsequently asked to lead the men of Lispole into Dingle in order to swell the parade assembled there to greet the men from Cahirciveen, who were coming to Dingle by boat. Parades were important as a means of the IRB making its presence known, as well as being a morale-booster. More importantly from Blythe's point of view, the meeting in Dingle proved to be the occasion of his first venture into public speaking. Blythe had never before made a speech in public, and he had no idea what he would say when he was invited to speak. But he had a topic ready to hand: the First World War had just begun. He recalls:

I heard myself saying that if the Germans came as enemies we would do our best to resist them, but that if they came to help us to throw off the English yoke we would flock to their standards. After a few other remarks, I called on the All-Merciful God to crown the German Eagles with victory. I noticed that the RIC who were present were looking as black as thunder, and I thought that they would move forward to arrest me.

Desmond FitzGerald was in the parade with fifty or sixty men from Ventry, and at the end of my first sentence he led them in a cheer. That was taken up by other groups and I was four or five times cheered by the whole crowd.

The speech attracted a great deal of attention; Blythe himself believed that it caused Sean McDermott to send for him to take up the post of organiser of the IRB. Blythe's first task as organiser was to swear in some new members: 'some men I could trust', as he put it. It was at this stage that he swore in Desmond FitzGerald, at the same time giving him the task of getting some men in Ventry.

Very soon, however, Sean McDermott wanted him for urgent work in the northern counties of Antrim, Derry, Donegal and Tyrone. Once more, he had to leave Kerry. His task in his new job was to seek out members of the old IRB in these four counties, with the purpose of building up the organisation there. Blythe found it almost impossible to kindle any spark of national feeling in the areas he traversed, mostly on his bicycle. He did indeed find some elderly men who had joined the IRB in the old days, but it seemed to him that all that remained of the old Fenian spirit was a deep dislike of the Hibernians and of the Parliamentary movement:

Apparently what had happened in that area (Toomebridge) and in adjoining areas across the river in County Derry ever since the Fenian time was that all the young fellows who had a National outlook were sworn into the IRB when they grew up, and that all of them, or practically all of them, left it when they got married.

He found a slight improvement, however, in Donegal and was approached by a man called Hugh McDuff, who asked him to address a meeting of interested people. Blythe recalls:

> We held the meeting in the dead of night in the middle of
> a bog. There seemed to be forty or fifty present.

It was while Blythe was working in the northern counties that he met Herbert Moore Pim, who was to become a friend of his. But on the whole, Blythe was glad to be taken off his work in the north. The Volunteer Executive appointed him as organiser for the Volunteers and he was requested to return to Dublin. Two other organisers – 'Ginger' O'Connell and Liam Mellows – had been appointed at the same time, and each man was given his own area. The area assigned to Blythe was Counties Cork, Kerry, Limerick and Clare.

Early in the new year of 1915, he set out to organise the volunteers in County Cork. He could spend only a few weeks on this task. He travelled around the counties, making contact with men whose names he had been given. But generally speaking, it was a most dispiriting exercise. Only a few months before, the Volunteer movement had been split into two unequal parts by the leader of the Irish Parliamentary Party, John Redmond. This event troubled most of the witnesses who gave evidence to the Bureau of Military History. It complicated the lives of the Volunteer organisers, who were attempting to resurrect a deeply damaged movement. In town after town, it was the same story. Despite the fact that his contacts might be strong Sinn Féiners, he found recruitment hard going. In Fermoy, for example, where he had been given the name of a barber, he:

> could find nobody . . . who was prepared to make any move
> towards forming a Company of Irish Volunteers. Generally
> speaking, the position in County Cork was nearly as bad as
> it could be.

He found the response in Kerry somewhat better, particularly in the Dingle and Tralee area, where he had lived. He then went to Limerick, where the Volunteers were already better organised than in either Kerry or Cork. The Volunteers in Limerick operated under the control of a County Executive based in Limerick city, of which the president was one Father Wall. Their drill instructor was Robert Monteith, who later became better known for his part in the landing of Roger Casement on Banna Strand in Kerry.

Blythe then moved on to Clare. In each county area, he noticed that he was much better received in the country areas outside the towns. Although progress was slow in Clare in 1915, the mood gradually changed:

> I went over, I think, every part of County Limerick between my return about November and the middle of March 1916, and while one could not say that a Volunteer Company was formed in every parish, it was clear that it would not be long until that was the position.

According to Blythe, County Clare was slower than other counties to get going, but as the year progressed he was able to establish several Companies of Volunteers there.

Blythe's career as an organiser for the Irish Volunteers came to an abrupt end in a small hotel in Athea in the early hours of one morning in March 1916, when he was arrested by the District Inspector. His arrest cannot have come as a surprise to him. He had been served with an order to leave Ireland the previous July and had been given the choice of two or three places in England to which he would be deported. Time had run out for Blythe: he spent Easter Week in Abingdon and missed the Rising.

Not everyone in County Clare would agree with Ernest Blythe's sometimes harsh assessment of the state of national feeling there and in the surrounding counties. Joe Barrett from Kilrush in County Clare was able to give an insider's view of the state of the IRB in County Clare dating back to 15 August 1908, when he was sworn into the Fenian Brotherhood.

Barrett was born in February 1888, at Barnageeha, Darragh, Ennis, County Clare. He was the eldest of a family of sixteen, consisting of ten boys and six girls. He worked on his father's farm after leaving Killone National School. At the time Barrett joined the IRB:

> It was the practice in our part of Clare to invite the eldest son of all the old Fenians to become members of the Brotherhood, and my father was an old Fenian at the time. I was sworn in by Peter McInerney of Lisheen, Ballynacally, County Clare, at an unoccupied house at Drumquin. There were fifteen of us, mostly the eldest sons of old Fenians, sworn in on the same night. This fifteen formed the nucleus of a Circle which represented three or four parishes. We held meetings about every two months or so, where the ways and means of procuring arms and ammunition were discussed and, so far as we were able, we did our best to acquire what arms we could.

According to Barrett, the Circle grew: between 1909 and 1913, it extended its membership throughout County Clare, 'especially within the radius of ten or fifteen miles from the town of Ennis, which came to be the meeting place for the members of that Circle.'

In 1913, after the Irish Volunteer organisation had been started in Dublin, Barrett and his friends organised a Company of Volunteers in County Clare:

> without assistance or instructions from any outside body or person, that is to say, we had no instructions from the Supreme Council, on the one hand, or the newly formed Volunteer Executive, on the other. Between the end of 1913 and the summer of 1914, Volunteer companies were started in most parishes in Clare.

By the time Blythe arrived in County Clare, the situation had changed. The Redmond split (described in the next chapter) affected the whole country, including County Clare, where William Redmond, then head of the Irish Parliamentary Party, was the MP for East Clare. In June or July 1914, Redmond reviewed a parade of the Irish Volunteers in Ennis. A few months later, the Irish Parliamentary Party was urging the Volunteers to 'join the British army and fight for England' in the war.

This was deeply disturbing for people like Joe Barrett and Ernest Blythe. For a time, matters did not go well for the Irish Volunteers. But as 1915 wore on, a number of Redmondite Volunteers rejoined the Irish Volunteers. Arms were being procured in various ways. For instance, soldiers were coming home on leave at the time and were allowed to carry their rifles and equipment into their homes. In almost all cases, these arms were collected by the Volunteers. Sometimes they simply took the rifles; on other occasions, they were able to get them for the price of a few drinks. Soon the British army stopped the practice of allowing the soldiers to bring their rifles home while on leave.

Barrett refers to Blythe's time in County Clare in one short paragraph:

> During 1915 Ernest Blythe came to Clare as an Irish Volunteer organiser – a job which he carried out very satis- factorily. He was followed everywhere he went by the RIC, frequently eluding them and leading them on wild goose chases, to his great amusement. The RIC authorities in Clare at the time visited the hotels which had given him accommodation and asked the proprietors not to keep him. In this request, the police were generally successful, and Blythe was only able to get accommodation in an odd hotel here and there.

4

'THE WHOLE THING BROKE UP'

By the time these testimonies came to be written, it had become something of a marvel to the people concerned that they had actually taken part in the Rising. In the first place, it was not until afterwards that they realised how it had very nearly not happened, and secondly, they realised how close they had come to missing it themselves. One young person who missed the Rising was Eileen McGrane (later Mrs McCarville), who was a student of Tom MacDonagh's in 1916, living in Loreto Hall, a convent hostel where she often felt out of things:

> I was on holidays in Kildare during Easter Week. When I heard of the Rising, I came to Dublin by train on Easter Monday. I had an idea of getting in touch with Tom MacDonagh, who was the only one I knew that would be in the Rising. I did not succeed and went back to Kildare, getting a lift on a lorry.

Poor Eileen McGrane would not have been involved in much beyond her studies. Other young people were in the thick of things. There was the Gaelic League, of course, which was meant to be mainly a cultural organisation but, as so many witnesses experienced, provided its members with the opportunity to discuss the politics and other issues of the day. Then there was Cumann na mBan, and the Irish Volunteers. Finally, there was the Citizen Army, which in the words of Nora Connolly O'Brien had its origins in the Lockout of 1913:

Out of the Strike then, the Citizen Army was born. They did their drilling with broom handles and hurley sticks. I remember seeing Captain White training them in Croydon Park.

It was at this time that Nora Connolly O'Brien went to Belfast to form Cumann na mBan.

The Irish Volunteers became so successful that the Irish Parliamentary Party, whose members thought it had Home Rule within its grasp at last, became worried. Their leader, John Redmond, moved quickly to gain control of the national movement. He issued a manifesto which demanded that the Irish Volunteers expand their committee to give the Irish Parliamentary Party a controlling interest in the movement. Amazingly, the Volunteer leaders consented. Sean McGarry describes the impact of this move on the old Fenian Tom Clarke, a key figure of the Rising:

> I was with Tom when the news came, and to say he was astounded is understating it. I never saw him so moved. He regarded it from the beginning as cold-blooded and contemplated treachery likely to bring about the destruction of the only movement in a century which brought promise of all his hopes.

A split was inevitable, and it came when Redmond felt that he had to deliver something in return for Home Rule, at the same time as securing Home Rule against the opposition of Ulster unionists. In 1914, the Great War broke out, and Home Rule was put on ice. Britain was desperate for recruits to the British army to engage in the contest which lay ahead. The Ulster Volunteers rallied to the flag. Redmond, on 20 September 1914, did likewise, and received overwhelming support from nationalists. Every part of the country was affected by Redmond's action – none more so than the northern counties, as the organisers of the Volunteers, such as Ernest Blythe, could testify. The account by Seamus Dobbyn, a member of the IRB Supreme Council from 1917 to 1921, gives us a rare insight into the passions and struggles of the minority nationalist community in Belfast:

At the time of the Split, meetings were called all over Ireland, and our meeting was called and held in St Mary's Hall, Belfast. Joe Devlin, MP, presided. He made his statement, giving the Redmondite view of the policy of the Volunteers, which briefly was the same as Redmond had indicated in the famous Woodenbridge speech, where he had called on the Volunteers to aid England in the war against Germany in the so-called fight for small nations. Joe Devlin then called on Denis McCullough to give the views of the opposition. McCullough made many attempts to get his statement across, but was booed down by a patently packed meeting. Devlin made a couple of obviously feeble attempts to get him a hearing, but each time called on Mr McCullough not to say anything that would hurt the feelings of the majority at the meeting.

Soon afterwards, Denis McCullough left the meeting, taking his supporters with him. They settled down to 'military training, rifle practice – mostly miniature rifle practice – and field drill. This continued right up to the Rising,' Dobbyn noted.

In Dundalk, where Sean MacEntee had been a member of the Volunteers from the time of their first meeting:

> After the outbreak of the war and Redmond's recruiting speech, the whole thing broke up because Dundalk became a great recruiting town, as the Hibernians became a very strong force there.

But MacEntee and his friends reorganised the Volunteers in Dundalk, and like the small group in Belfast they began to drill regularly. Besides the Rising, they now had a new objective – to get hold of the 'Redmondite rifles'. MacEntee almost missed the Rising because of these rifles. Like him, most of the veteran Volunteers who gave testimony grieved for the loss of the rifles rather more than they did for the departure of the many men who followed Redmond.

Commandant General Boylan maintains that he foresaw something of the kind from the beginning:

> When the Irish Volunteers were started in Dunboyne some-
> time in 1914, I and some thirty others did not join. My rea-
> son for this was that I had no faith in the Irish Volunteers
> as then constituted. I knew that most of the men, and par-
> ticularly the influential ones amongst them, would never
> fight for Irish freedom. Instead, we formed our own dis-
> tinct Volunteer Unit and had no connection with the local
> 'Irish Volunteers', as they then were. I started this separate
> Volunteer Unit. We did not ask our members to take any
> oath on joining.

General Boylan's action was not as unusual as he might have
thought it was. There were a few others who determined their own
route to revolution.

Joseph Scollan came to Dublin from Derry in 1911, long before
Edward Carson resurrected the newly regenerated Ulster
Volunteers. Scollan had been appointed National Director of the
Ancient Order of Hibernians, and in the course of his reading of
the constitution of the American counterpart of the Ancient Order
of Hibernians:

> we found provision for an organisation of a military nature.
> This comprised one Company of men organised on a mil-
> itary basis in each Division. There were three divisions of
> the order in Dublin. The 'Red Hand' in Pearse Street,
> 'Clann na Gael' in Parliament Street and 'O'Connell'
> Division in Rathfarnham.
>   I decided to organise a company in each Division to be
> known as Hibernian Rifles which corresponded to the
> American organisation.

Scollan succeeded in building up a small force of carefully
selected men in 1912 and 1913. Ex-British army men provided a
plentiful supply of army instructors and were able to engage in a

great deal of foot drill and military exercises. In 1913, most of Scollan's members were connected with the Lockout; when he appealed to his friends in the Ancient Order of Hibernians American Alliance in the United States for funds to help these members, they sent $1,000, which was used to augment whatever strike pay the trade unions could manage. When Edward Carson began to organise his Volunteers in the north, Scollan felt the lack of arms keenly. There was a limit to what they could do with broom handles for training in the use of rifles. He wrote to America asking the organisation there to supply the Irish divisions with arms. The generosity of the Americans did not, however, extend to providing arms, and they had to make do with the broom handles. All the Volunteers got of a military nature was a supply of American military textbooks: these were not what Scollan had had in mind.

Neither the outbreak of war in 1914 nor the mass defection of Redmondites affected the Hibernians to any great extent. They had always kept themselves aloof from the Irish Volunteers. Certain members of the Executive of the Volunteers 'were not acceptable to our members as they had taken a prominent part in the Labour dispute on the "Masters" side,' Scollan recalls.

The Hibernian Rifles were very much closer to the Citizen Army than the Volunteers were; in 1915, Scollan did a deal with James Connolly. Connolly had some Italian rifles on hand for the use of his Citizen Army but needed money badly. He was in possession of information regarding the building of 'Q' ships (armed and disguised merchant ships that were used as decoys or to destroy submarines) in Belfast and wanted to get this information to the German ambassador in the United States. The safest way to do this was to send his daughter to inform the ambassador, and he needed the money for the passage. Scollan agreed to buy thirty rifles from him for £30. Connolly's daughter, Nora, got to America and delivered the message. The only snag was that the rifles were of little use to the Hibernians: they were Italian, and no ammunition could be found for them. Nothing daunted, Scollan continued his preparations, buying rifles when he could from the British army. He had bought about a hundred rifles from the Enniskillen Fusiliers when they had been stationed in Dollymount in 1914. The Hibernian

Rifles modified blank ammunition which they had bought from British soldiers, and were able to lay their hands on some shotguns. They waited for the call.

Others came to the Rising in a less formal manner. James Foran, from Crumlin in Dublin, had joined the Volunteers in 1915. He got things clear at the outset:

> I went up to [the Volunteer camp at] Larkfield and saw [Thomas] MacDonagh and Seamus Murphy, and I asked them did they intend to fight. They told me that they did intend to fight and that they probably would. I said, in that case I wanted to join. I said that I did not want to attend parades, that I had a big family, but that I would come up an odd time.

James Foran had a thriving painting business, with five or six men working for him in Charlemont Street. He lived in a big house on the corner of Rutland Avenue, which was convenient to Larkfield House, where men of military age from Britain were accommodated. (Larkfield House was the Plunkett family estate; the substantial body of IRB men stationed there were known as the Kimmage Garrison.) They had come over early in 1916 and were known IRB, according to Seamus Robinson, who had come over from Glasgow shortly after February 1916. Immediately on recruitment to the organisation, Robinson was informed that all young men of military age were required in Ireland:

> Our activities at Kimmage were mainly confined to the making of munitions under continuous armed guard. Our work consisted mostly of making buckshot for cartridges and cases for home-made bombs and grenades.

George Plunkett was Officer Commanding. True to his word, Foran kept going to the odd parade. But it would have been wiser for him to have kept in closer contact with his Company:

One morning during the week before Easter Week I was in bed and it started to rain, I think it was Monday morning of Holy Week 1916. One of the children – they were all young at the time – ran up the stairs and said to me, 'Daddy, the soldiers are in the yard. The yard is full of them.' I said, 'They are coming very quickly. I'll get up.' I thought they were coming to arrest me, because there were rumours at that time that we were going to be arrested and all that kind of thing.

Foran found the shed full of soldiers. He managed to have a friendly conversation with the officer in charge. It seemed that the soldiers were just standing in out of the rain. He told them that they were quite welcome and expressed the hope that they would put a stop to those 'fellows playing with their guns'. The officer undertook to do so. In fact, the soldiers were making a sketch of the area, including Larkfield.

That night, Foran was pleased to be able to report his conversation to Éamonn Ceannt. The Easter Sunday parade passed off normally, and although he had his suspicions that something was up, he heard nothing definite until the next day:

On Monday morning I brought my brother-in-law, whose name was Donnelly, up along Rutland Avenue to show him where the Liverpool fellows had their place. They had a forge there for making their pike-heads. When we got up everything was cleared out, the forge and everything else was gone. That was about half past ten in the morning. I did not know what was up and I said, 'They are all gone.' Just then up came Cathal Brugha on a bicycle. I said to him, 'What is the trouble? They are all gone away.' He said, 'They are all gone.' 'Is the fight on now?' said I. 'Yes,' said he. 'Right,' I said. Then he said, 'What way are you going?' 'I am going back to the Barn [Dolphin's Barn],' said I. 'Do you know where Ceannt lives?' said he. 'I do,' said I. 'Will you take a note to him? Take my bicycle and be as quick as you can.' I said to my brother-in-law, 'Goodbye, and if anything

happens to me will you look after the wife and kids?'
'Right,' said he.

I got up on the bicycle and away I went as straight as a die to [Éamonn] Ceannt's house.

Foran was on track again for the Rising after having almost missed it. He accompanied Ceannt to Emerald Square.

'CERTAIN BIG EVENTS'

A number of the witnesses say that they knew the Rising was coming as Easter approached. Tom Harris from Prosperous was alerted early in Holy Week:

> On Spy Wednesday of 1916, a young fellow named Sweeney came out from Naas with a despatch to tell me to go to Newbridge, that Lieutenant O'Kelly wanted to see me there. I was in Newbridge about 12 or 1 o'clock. That was the first time I met Tom Byrne. Tom had fought with the Boers in the South African War. They informed me that the Rising would take place anytime within the next week and that arms were on their way from Germany.

Monsignor Paddy Browne, a member of the staff of Maynooth College, remembered that he went to his mother's in County Tipperary on the same day, but not surprisingly he:

> had not the slightest notion that anything was going to happen. I did not know anything about dispatches going about the country.
>
> About a fortnight before I left Maynooth on holidays, Sean McDermott and Charlie Power visited me in Maynooth. They stayed the night. We played bridge – Dr Denaghy being the fourth player – for the most of the night and they did not leave until the next morning by the early train. On that occasion there was no talk, as far as I can recollect, no mention of the Rising.

Con O'Donovan, a student from Cork, remembered:

The week previous to Easter Sunday, I should have been at home in Cork on holidays, and it was Piaras Beasley clenched my decision to stay in Dublin. As a result, I was available all that week as carrier of dispatches, messages and, at times, heavier goods.

For about a fortnight before Easter, Dr Kathleen Lynn was kept busy ferrying members of the Citizen Army, and arms and ammunition. Dr Lynn remembered:

One night in Holy Week I went out with the car to St Enda's, and there they loaded it up with ammunition and put some theatrical stuff on top of it, hoping to get through. Willie Pearse and I brought it in and landed it safely in Liberty Hall, where there were many willing hands to unload it.

On another night – I think it was the Friday before Palm Sunday – Dr McNabb brought down a carload of ammunition from Belfast and dumped it at the back of my house. That was stuff for the Volunteers, who removed it all on the Saturday night.

Dr Lynn knew well that a Rising was imminent:

I think it was not until Saturday that I knew where I was assigned to for the Rising.

Min Ryan remembered that:

For little more than a week before the Rising, there was tremendous excitement – a sort of seething undercurrent. You felt that something was going to happen, but what it was you did not know. . . . Our rooms were entirely given over to bandage-making at that time. There were supposed to be great Easter manoeuvres to show our strength. We felt that, although there had been manoeuvres, this was something different.

73

Every year, the Ryan sisters and their brother Jim (later Dr Jim Ryan TD, Minister for Health and Minister for Social Welfare) went home to the family farm at Tomcoole, County Wexford, for Easter. This year, when Sean McDermott heard that Min planned to go to Tomcoole as usual, he asked her not to. 'You ought to remain in Dublin over Easter with Jim,' he said. 'Jim is under orders. You ought to stay and look after him.'

Min decided to remain in Dublin over Easter. She took a written despatch to Wexford on Holy Thursday morning for delivery to the Volunteers there. She was back in Dublin on the evening of that day.

Sean McDermott had numerous messages to send. The first lot of despatches were on their way. Charles Wyse-Power, who lived very close to the centre of the city, clearly remembered the part he played:

> Early in that week, I think on Tuesday, I came home to 21 Henry Street and suddenly I found Sean standing beside me. I can't say whether he was attending a meeting at the house or whether he had come from somewhere else. He told me he wanted me to go to Limerick by the 6 o'clock train that evening with a despatch for John Daly. He handed me an envelope, which he said contained £50 in banknotes. I don't know what else was in the envelope. He also gave me a verbal message. He told me if there was any danger of my being searched on the journey, I was to get rid of the envelope and its contents through the window, but I was to keep the message in my head. The verbal message was: 'The wireless stuff will be landed at Cahirciveen'.

When Wyse-Power reached John Daly's in Limerick, he had to wait for a while until a couple of RIC men, who were patrolling nearby, left the area. When he got to John Daly's house, his message was taken from him by Sean O'Muirthuille and Sean FitzGibbon, who came downstairs to receive it. At about 1 o'clock, these two men came down again, accompanied by a man called Colivet. Wyse-Power was immediately given the task of bringing Colivet back with him to Dublin the next morning. He had to take the first train.

Wyse-Power tried to pinpoint these dates when he made his statement:

> I feel fairly sure it was Tuesday I went to Limerick and that
> I returned on Wednesday, as I have a distinct recollection of
> not going to Mass on Holy Thursday and that I could have
> done.

Wyse-Power was aware that his part was linked to the whole Casement enterprise and the ill-fated German connection.

Linked too to the Casement debacle was Mairín Cregan, who, like her friends the Ryans from Tomcoole, intended to go home for the Easter holidays. She planned to take the morning train on Holy Thursday, but on the afternoon of Spy Wednesday she got a message that Sean McDermott wanted to see her before she left:

> Later that evening, a young man, a stranger to me – I heard
> later that his name was Cullen – arrived and gave me some
> automatics and ammunition, saying that he was told to give
> them to me for delivery to the Volunteers in Tralee. . . . I
> think it was almost midnight when Sean McDermott and
> Gearoid O'Sullivan arrived. Miss K. Brady and Jim Ryan,
> medical student and Volunteer, were with me.

Out of earshot of the rest, Sean McDermott gave Cregan detailed instructions. As soon as she arrived in Tralee, she was to go to Father Breen, who would put her in touch with Austin Stack and Paddy Cahill. She was to give them the automatics and the ammunition, as well as the letters. She carried out her instructions. Father Breen sent two boys with her to the skating rink, where she found Austin Stack, Paddy Cahill and the rest. They were not skating; they were manufacturing bombs and bullets. One of the letters she was carrying was a request to a family by the name of Quinlan for help in landing the arms, which were to arrive in Kerry 'one of these days,' as Cregan put it.

It so happened that Cregan was back home in Killorglin when:

At about ten o'clock on Good Friday evening, as I was preparing for bed, news spread through the town of Killorglin that a car had gone over Ballykissane Quay. With my sister I went there and managed to get hold of Tommy McInerney, driver of the car and the only one saved.

Cregan immediately grasped the significance of the event and set about limiting the damage to the whole project which would follow questioning by the police. Her first task was to win McInerney's trust. He placed himself in her hands; her friends were able to postpone his arrest and, more importantly, take his revolver and hide it. Cregan remained in Kerry.

Con Keating, a wireless operator, was one of those drowned in the car which went off the quay at Ballykissane. He had with him a lamp which he had received from Éamonn Ceannt. The lamp was to have been used to signal to the German ship the *Aud*, which was to carry arms to Ireland for the Rising.

Aine Ceannt, the widow of Éamonn Ceannt, could remember well the events of those last weeks before the Rising. She was in a good position to be able to do so: in January 1916, the Military Council had begun to meet at the Ceannt house. She recalls:

> Only on the first occasion did I meet the Council, and then I met Clarke, McDermott and Pearse. I have no recollection of meeting Joe Plunkett at that meeting, although he was probably there.

She also describes the unique method by which James Connolly would announce his call to arms to the men of the Citizen Army:

> Connolly had instructed his next-in-command that if at any time he disappeared and did not turn up within three days, the Citizen Army was to go out and take Dublin Castle.

Connolly disappeared towards the end of January but was persuaded to hold off on the military action. The crisis passed, and Connolly reappeared:

At the next meeting of the Military Council, held at our house, Connolly was present and was a member of that body from that day forward.

Frank Robbins gives an alternative version of Connolly's disappearance in early 1916. According to this account, the disappearance may not have been voluntary; it would appear to have been closer to a kidnapping. In 1916, Robbins was a sergeant in the Citizen Army. In his testimony, he recounts a conversation he had with Michael Mallin, who was second-in-command to Connolly:

> Mallin then went on to tell me about Connolly's disappearance. He said that Connolly disappeared for a number of days, nobody knew where, nor could any information be obtained as to his whereabouts. Mallin came to the conclusion that as there had been strained relations between Connolly and leading members of the IRB, who had charge of the Irish Volunteer Organisation and were very annoyed at Connolly's criticism of their policy, that they had all to do with his disappearance.

We do not have a statement from Mallin, who was one of those executed for his part in the Rising, but Robbins gives a dramatic account, as described to him, of the confrontation between Mallin and the Military Council on Good Friday 1916 between 11 AM and 12 noon. Robbins then gives his own judgement on Connolly's disappearance:

> My own personal view of Connolly's disappearance is that he would not have left Liberty Hall of his own free will without informing Thomas Foran and William O'Brien that he was going away for a few days, knowing how concerned the officials then in charge of the union would be. Connolly was not a man to neglect his union duties, and would have made some arrangement for someone else to carry out those duties had he planned to be absent for any period of time. I am therefore convinced that his disappearance from Liberty Hall was because of some restraining force.

77

The Irishmen from London, Liverpool, Manchester and Glasgow who had returnd to Dublin in February knew why they had come. They waited at Larkfield preparing for the Rising. Members of Cumann na mBan were asked to procure as many old tweed suits as they could, to be converted into sleeping bags for the men.

By February 1916, many of the Volunteers, even those not living in Dublin, had a fair idea 'that something was definitely planned,' Sean MacEntee, who had been living and working in Dundalk since 1914, reports. By Holy Week, word was more definite, MacEntee remembers:

> On Holy Thursday afternoon Paddy Hughes came into my office at the Electricity Works, Dundalk.
>
> 'Mac,' said he, 'the word has come!'

On Holy Thursday night, MacEntee prepared himself for the Rising:

> That night I went to Belfast to bid goodbye to my family and to buy surgical bandages and first-aid satchels, some Ordnance maps, a pair of binoculars, a prismatic compass and such other items of an officer's paraphernalia as I could afford. On Saturday afternoon I returned to Dundalk.

In Dublin on that same Saturday, Éamonn and Aine Ceannt went out to Dalkey to ask a friend for the loan of field glasses. On the way out, on the top deck of the tram Éamonn whispered to Aine: 'The man who landed in Kerry was Roger Casement and the man who got away was Monteith. If they catch Monteith, they'll hang him.'

According to Sean McGarry's evidence, Tom Clarke was dead set against Casement's German expedition. Before Casement left for America, where he hoped to get a passport for Germany, Tom Clarke did his best to dissuade him from going. In spite of all Clarke's efforts, Casement made his way to Germany, where, it appears, he gave the Germans the idea that there could be no rising in Ireland unless the Germans landed an army. Joe Plunkett was sent to Germany forthwith – and in spite of illness was able to impress on the Germans that:

> the possibility of a German invasion was not even considered and that there would certainly be a rising.

Later, when Casement heard that the date of the Rising had been fixed, he thought that the Germans 'had deceived us, as he could not conceive that there would be a rising without an invasion, and he persuaded the German government to land him here with the results we all know,' McGarry notes.

As Easter Week approached, and before anything had been heard about Casement, McGarry tells us that any tension that he and his fellow Volunteers had felt early in the week seemed to have cleared up by about the middle of the week:

> McDermott called to my office on Wednesday in jubilant mood. He told me that everything was going well, that MacNeill had agreed to everything.
>
> On Friday news [came] that Con Keating, Sheahan and Monahan [first names not given], who had gone to make contact with the German ship, had been drowned, their car having run into a river in the darkness. There were tears in Tom's eyes as he told me. He had given the lads instructions on the previous day – and now they were dead.

Sean T. O'Kelly – who was President of Ireland when he dictated detailed and careful evidence over a period of some months in 1953 – was in a position to know almost everything that was going on in the national movement, particularly during the feverish weeks that immediately preceded the Rising. A lot of the activity concerned Eoin MacNeill. Sean T. O'Kelly tells us:

> I think it was on Sunday the 9th April 1916 that Sean McDermott asked me to go with him to Woodtown Park, Rathfarnham, where he said he was anxious to have a talk with MacNeill. He suggested that it would be a good idea if

we got two girls to accompany us just to throw off suspicion in case detectives were watching us, as they surely would be.

McDermott, O'Kelly and the two Ryan sisters, Min and Phyllis, went out to Woodtown. McDermott went in to talk to MacNeill, leaving the Ryan sisters and O'Kelly to wait in the car. When McDermott came out to rejoin them, he was in high good humour. Later, when they had:

parted from the ladies, he told me that he was very happy with the result of his interview; that he had a full, free and frank discussion with MacNeill as to coming events.

By 'coming events', O'Kelly understood McDermott to mean the Rising. It is important to remember that O'Kelly was aware that a decision had been taken in September 1914 that a rising would take place. In fact, he had been 'sent to America to give verbally a detailed account of the plans for the coming rising, at least as far as Dublin was concerned, which they [Clarke and McDermott] had imparted to me.'

But on 16 April, Sean McDermott asked Sean T. O'Kelly to accompany him again on a visit to see Eoin MacNeill. This time they took two 'lady friends' – not Phyllis and her sister Min this time, but Min and a friend, Miss Bridget Doheney. McDermott again went in alone and again came out well satisfied with the interview. This time, McDermott told O'Kelly a little more:

What I do remember is that McDermott went into great detail with me describing his talk with MacNeill. He said that MacNeill had been giving a great deal of trouble; that he had changed his mind several times; that when he had seen McDermott on the previous Sunday, MacNeill had accepted in full the programme that had been drawn up for Easter but that during the week others had discussed the matter with him and had persuaded him to change his mind . . . I well remember that McDermott said to me: 'I have discussed everything with MacNeill, every detail of the arrangements for Easter Sunday, and he has accepted all our plans. I hope to God that he does not run away again during the coming week. I'll have to see what we can do with those fellows who are interfering and influencing MacNeill and putting him in the wrong direction. I'll have to do something about it.

According to O'Kelly's account, Dublin was in a fever of activity during the coming week:

One would meet members of the Volunteers everywhere around the city who would tell one of their plans to arm and equip themselves so as to make as good as good a show as possible at the manoeuvres on the following Sunday. Shops like Lawlors of Fownes Street which made a speciality of selling Volunteer equipment were full from morning to night with Volunteers seeking to purchase equipment of various kinds.

O'Kelly clearly remembered that everywhere one went, the manoeuvres planned for the coming Sunday were the subject of intense discussion and excitement. Certainly he intended to take part in whatever was planned. Pearse had already appointed him to serve on his staff with the rank of Captain, to take effect 'when certain big events took place', as O'Kelly put it.

'Certain big events' were indeed imminent. On Saturday evening, Éamonn Ceannt told Aine that 'they would strike next day.' The flag of green, white and orange – to symbolise peace between the nationalists and unionists – which had been made earlier by Mrs Mellows, was sprinkled with holy water.

Simon Donnelly, who was to be promoted to captain of his Company on Easter Monday, had been an active member of the Volunteers since 1913. He joined the IRB in 1914 and had taken part in the Howth gun-running. He bought his first Martini rifle openly some time late in 1914. Donnelly recalls in his witness statement the training he received as a Volunteer:

The training all along consisted of routine close-order drill, marches and field days on Sundays.

The Volunteers were instructed by former British soldiers. Following the outbreak of the Great War, it became necessary to dismiss all ex-British soldiers from parades, for their own protection. Like many other witnesses, Donnelly describes the air of crisis and excitement hanging over the city in the weeks preceding Easter Week. Continuous lectures were given to junior officers at No. 2 Dawson Street at Volunteer headquarters. While attending one of these on Good Friday 1916, Donnelly was given a special task. He remembers that he was asked:

> to carry out certain work on the following Saturday, namely, the removal of arms from a dump in Exchange Street to be distributed throughout the area we were to occupy.
>
> My last recollection of the few hours spent in No. 2 Dawson Street was of a few junior officers, of whom I was one, having a sort of discussion and friendly chat with the late Thomas MacDonagh, who produced a large map of Dublin on which he had outlined the original plan of [Robert] Emmet for the defence of Dublin. I have no recollection of MacDonagh referring at any time to the positions which we were to occupy.

In his witness statement, Maurice J. Collins from Glasnevin remembered that he had made arrangements to travel to the country with his fiancée for the Easter weekend. He remembers:

> Jack Shouldice [a member of the IRB and Ernest Blythe's superior when the latter had worked as a boy clerk in the Department of Agriculture] called on Easter Saturday morning to tell me that the Rising was fixed for the following day – Easter Sunday. I then told him of the plans I had made to go to the country. His comment was, 'Well, Maurice, although you have arrangements made to go to the country, never deny that I did not tell you.' In reply I said, 'Certainly not, Jack, I will never deny it and now I will not travel to the country.'

Collins awaited further orders. Like others, he was called to a parade the next day; the parade was subsequently cancelled following the issuing of the countermanding order. Aine Ceannt's evidence casts some light on the reason for the caution and secrecy which surrounded the communication of orders. In reply to a question from her, Éamonn Ceannt said:

> that they could not risk telling the men that the fight will be tomorrow, as at the time of the Fenian Rising as soon as the men were told about it they thronged the churches for Confession, and the authorities, knowing a lot of the men, suspected that something was going to happen and immediately took action.

Despatches were the main means of communication between the officers and men of the Volunteers, and couriers were chosen carefully. James Ryan was selected twice to act as a courier during those fateful days:

> On Good Friday 1916, at lunch in the Red Bank restaurant, Sean McDermott asked me if I would take a despatch to Cork that evening. I was only too glad to get busy at something and readily agreed. I was told to report at his office in D'Olier Street during the afternoon and to be prepared to travel on the night train to Cork. When I arrived at his office, Sean McDermott asked if I was armed. I said yes. I had a revolver. He then handed me a despatch, which was to be delivered to Tomás MacCurtain in Cork. He said it was a very important message and that I should prevent it from falling into hostile hands, even if I had to use the revolver to do so. He told me to destroy the message if necessary.
>
> I had never been in Cork.

It was about 4 AM on the morning of Saturday 22 April, the day before Easter Sunday, when Ryan arrived in Cork. The place was deserted. He approached two policemen, a sergeant and a constable, for help in finding a place to sleep. In the course of casual conversation with the sergeant, Jim Ryan learned that Roger Casement had been captured. Later, with the help of a friendly jarvey, he found MacCurtain and Terence MacSwiney in consultation with Captain J. J. O'Connell. He handed over the despatch to MacCurtain:

> The pith of the message was that agreement had been reached in Dublin and that the Rising was going ahead.

Thirty-one years later, in the course of his testimony, Dr Ryan was emphatic that the Volunteers were ready and anxious to fight in Cork and that they were not waiting for German arms. The message that Jim Ryan got from MacCurtain was: 'Tell Sean we will blaze away as long as the stuff lasts.' Dr Ryan took it that, by 'stuff', MacCurtain meant the arms they had to hand.

Ryan appears to have finished all his business in about four hours. He left Cork for Dublin at about 8 AM on the same morning. When he went to Sean McDermott to report the delivery of the despatch and to convey MacCurtain's reply, he found that he had to take his place in a queue: others also had to make their reports. It was late in the evening before McDermott got to see him. They walked down town together, accompanied by Gearoid O'Sullivan. Before they parted at Carlisle Bridge (now O'Connell Bridge), McDermott instructed him and Gearoid O'Sullivan to report to him at Liberty Hall the next day. The two were to be his personal staff. All was set for the next day. But before Ryan could get a night's sleep, the carefully laid plans were scuttled. Eoin MacNeill called a meeting at Dr Seamus Kelly's house at 54 Rathgar Road.

6

'SOMETHING MUST BE DONE'

On Holy Saturday, Min Ryan, who had come back from Wexford to be with her brother Jim, found herself sitting in the house at 19 Ranelagh Road wondering where everybody was. She recalls:

Anyway, on Holy Saturday afternoon about 3 or 4 o'clock, Sean T. [O'Kelly] came in and said he had been in with [Arthur] Griffith, who told him the Volunteers were going to rise the next morning. He must have told me that the IRB were very much behind the project and that the arms had been lost, that Sean FitzGibbon had come from Kerry and told [Eoin] MacNeill about the disaster. I am certain that it was Easter Saturday afternoon that Sean T. O'Kelly told me that. We talked it over and both of us felt that something must be done. He said 'I think I will go and see MacNeill.' So Sean T. went to see MacNeill. I had an uneasy feeling. We had not seen Sean McDermott. I thought that Sean T. would have been a big man in the IRB but at this stage I realised, to my surprise, that he was not. Sean T. came back from MacNeill afterwards and said that they were having a meeting that night in Dr Seamus O'Kelly's at 54 Rathgar Road, and that MacNeill would issue some statement. Sean T. was very upset about the whole situation as he was very much in the dark about things and he feared that the Rising might end in a holocaust.

He arranged with me to bring everyone we could find suitable up to Seamus O'Kelly's that evening in case the meeting wished to issue any message.

The young couriers waited outside the large room where the 'Volunteer people', who included Eoin MacNeill, Sean T. O'Kelly, Sean FitzGibbon and Cathal Brugha, met. Thomas McDonagh may have been there but Min Ryan wasn't sure. The meeting went on far into the night. The young Jim Ryan, who was one of the 'suitable' people recruited by his sister in case they were needed to deliver despatches, takes up the story:

> After some time the door of the meeting room opened and Eoin MacNeill appeared. He asked me if I had carried a despatch to Cork the previous day and if I knew where to find the leaders there. I answered yes to both questions. Good! Well, I was now to go to Cork again, this time by motor. It was urgent and I must deliver these despatches as soon as possible. In his hand he held five or six slips of paper, each in identical terms and signed by him. I was to deliver one to Pierce McCann in Tipperary, one to MacCurtain in Cork, one to the OC [Officer Commanding] in Tralee, if possible, and the remainder to officers of any groups of Volunteers I might see on parade during the journey.
>
> Eoin MacNeill's brother, James, driving his own car, and I left Dublin on this mission about midnight on Easter Saturday.

The message – in MacNeill's hand – which each courier had handed to them, was clear and unambiguous:

> There will be no manouvres tomorrow. All manouvres are cancelled. This is to be obeyed by every officer.

The message was signed by MacNeill. An order cancelling the manouvres had already been issued to the press.

Jim Ryan and James MacNeill reached Pierce MacCann's place in Tipperary at 6 AM and gave him the order. He was very surprised, 'as he said he had been speaking to MacNeill on Thursday,' Ryan reports, 'and he [MacNeill] was then in favour of the Rising.'

The two men continued on to Cork, where they met both Terence MacSweeney and Tomás MacCurtain. They got the impression that the Corkmen were not surprised by the changed orders. Ryan and MacNeill, who were under orders to get to Tralee, resumed their journey. They made it as far as Ballyvourney, County Cork, when their car broke down.They abandoned all hope of getting to Tralee. Ryan continues:

> On Easter Monday morning they decided that James MacNeill would remain over in Macroom to get the car repaired and I would get a train back to Dublin. The train stopped at Port Laoighse, where I learned there was fighting in Dublin, and further progress by train was impossible. Travelling partly on foot, partly by motor and partly by horse and jaunting car, I arrived in Dublin on Tuesday afternoon and reported to Sean MacDermott at the GPO.

Min Ryan was asked whether she would she go to Wexford; she waited until the next morning. According to her statement, O'Kelly walked her home after the Rathgar meeting but stayed outside 'on our road for I don't know how long' talking to Cathal Brugha, who was passionate in his efforts to overturn MacNeill's decision. O'Kelly turned up to the Rising, whatever about the misgivings Min Ryan believed he had about it.

On Easter Sunday morning, Min Ryan got off the train at Enniscorthy in order to deliver MacNeill's message to Ginger O'Connell, the officer in charge of the Volunteers in Wexford, Kilkenny and Carlow. O'Connell was devastated by the message and sat with his head in his hands. She explained some of the background to MacNeill's decision, insofar as she knew it. But she also said in her statement: 'My opinion is that there will be a Rising.' She knew Sean McDermott was at the back of the planned rising. She had not talked to him for some days, but she felt he would not abandon it. Later, when she went home to her family at Tomcoole, County Wexford, she kept saying: ' I am certain it will come off. I have to go back. I must go back to Dublin.' She went back to Dublin – by taxi – with her sister Phyllis. The taxi cost them £6 – a substantial sum of money at that time.

Next morning, Easter Monday, Min Ryan received a mobilisation order from Cumann na mBan and reported for duty to the

Broadstone area. They worked, possibly rolling bandages, all day on Monday, but in the evening they were no longer required. She and her friend Effie Taaffe made for O'Connell Street and the GPO:

> Then near the O'Connell Monument we saw Sean T. O'Kelly marching along with a little band of Citizen Army men. I had left Sean T. and Liam O'Brien in the house. They had both gone off and joined. Sean T. had come down to the GPO and met Pearse, who made him a Staff Captain. Liam O'Brien went in to the College of Surgeons and joined up with the Citizen Army there. And here was Sean T. leading that little band of men from the O'Connell Monument. He had about seven or eight fellows behind him. They were an odd number, I remember. So, 'Halt' came from Sean T. He was not in uniform but had a Sam Browne belt. Anyway, we stopped and said we had been disbanded. Then Sean T. said with that great air of his: 'Would you like to come into the Post Office? Would you like to see Sean McDermott?' I said: 'We would love that, but we were afraid to go in.' Sean T. said: 'Come along with me.'

And they followed him into the GPO.

In Dundalk, Sean MacEntee was having considerable difficulty in recovering the 'Redmondite' rifles (those of which former British soldiers had been 'relieved'). Just as he and his friends were about to break into the premises where the rifles were stored, the messenger from Dublin arrived to tell them that the Rising was off. But the main body of Volunteers had already left. MacEntee realised he had to get word to them: 'At any cost the Volunteers must be turned back,' he recalls in his statement. MacEntee searched the town for a motor car, but none was to be had, so he sent four messengers on bicycles. No sooner had they left than two cars became available. MacEntee left Dundalk for Slane in one of these cars and found his men. All was so quiet in Slane that he was convinced that there would indeed be no Rising. Not everyone agreed, however: one Patrick Hughes refused to believe that the countermanding order was genuine. Hughes and MacEntee talked long and earnestly about this turn of events and decided to sleep on it. The rain fell in a steady downpour most of the night.

Next morning, MacEntee caught the mail train at Drogheda at a quarter to four in the morning. He must get definite instructions. It was six o'clock on Sunday morning when he reached Dublin. He made his way to Liberty Hall.

The matter was far from clear in Dublin either, even on Sunday morning, when the *Sunday Independent* went on sale and everyone could read MacNeill's countermanding order. Sean McGarry describes the situation as follows:

> The worst blow of all was to come. It was the *Independent* of Easter Sunday. I had stayed with Tom in O'Mahoney's Hotel on Saturday night and left for early Mass on Sunday morning. On my way home I got the paper and read the order countermanding the mobilisation. I walked home in a daze to find Mick Collins, who had been staying with Plunkett and who came after Mass to breakfast in my house. I showed him the paper. He became dumb. We breakfasted in silence and left for Liberty Hall, where we found the Military Council was in session. . . . I found Tom Clarke afterwards and for the first time since I knew him he seemed crushed. He was weary and seemed crestfallen.

The boys from St Enda's got a copy too, before they attended First Mass. Eamon Bulfin, a lieutenant in the Rathfarnham Company, writes in his statement that:

> While standing outside the chapel after Mass, Mr MacNeill and Sean FitzGibbon approached me and asked me to carry a dispatch. I immediately came to the conclusion that this despatch was a part of the calling off of the manouvres, and I refused to take it. Mr MacNeill then called over Frank Connolly and he asked him to take the despatch for him. As far as I know, Frank Connolly did take the despatch for him, because he did not turn out with us on Easter Monday.

Thirty years on, the participants were still greatly concerned with the countermanding order and by the action taken by MacNeill. Nonetheless, their statements were in the main more concerned with the way in which the contradictory orders impinged on them personally, rather than on any analysis of MacNeill's motivation. Aine Ceannt's account is an exception in this respect:

> We discussed the effect of the countermanding order, and Éamonn said that the Volunteers would have agreed to majority rule, but that the order had been issued to the Press without their knowledge and without their having been consulted, therefore they should go ahead with their plans. I understood from Éamonn that at first John [Eoin] MacNeill was tardy about agreeing to the Rising. He then agreed and orders were issued throughout the country. He was inclined to wobble again, but Thomas said to Éamonn, when coming back from the meeting in Dundrum on Thursday, 'I believe MacNeill will be all right if we can keep him away from . . . ' (Mrs Ceannt does not wish to disclose the name of this person.) He added, 'As soon as we start I feel certain that MacNeill will be with us.'

Aine Ceannt goes on to give the most likely explanation for the issuing of the countermanding order. She says:

> In justification, possibly, of Eoin MacNeill's action it must be recorded that the messenger who had been sent down to superintend the distribution of the guns which were to arrive on the *Aud* had returned hastily to Dublin, and reported to Mr MacNeill that the *Aud* carrying the guns had been scuttled. MacNeill hurriedly called together some sympathisers with the movement, but I would not put them down as prominent Volunteers. In his haste to prevent, as he thought, a failure, he omitted to call the strong men into consultation.
>
> After the order cancelling the manouvres had been actually given to the Press, as far as I know, Thomas MacDonagh was summoned to give his opinion on the

matter. I was informed that when Mr MacNeill asked Commandant MacDonagh for his opinion, MacDonagh looked around and replied ' I owe no counsel to these men' and left the house. He then sought Cathal Brugha, who lived in the neighbourhood, and I understand that Cathal interviewed MacNeill and was very angry with him. He, Cathal, then made his way to [Éamonn Ceannt's] house and told him what had occurred. In his excitement he omitted to say *which* O'Kelly's house was the venue for the meeting.

Sean T. O'Kelly gives a much stronger account of the encounter between Thomas MacDonagh and Eoin MacNeill at Dr O'Kelly's house that Saturday night in Rathgar, when Eoin MacNeill told MacDonagh what he had decided to do – indeed, what he had already done – in parts of the country:

That is that he had sent out orders countermanding the manoeuvres.

MacDonagh then, in my hearing, said to him that he, MacNeill, had full knowledge of all that was intended to take place that week, and that he had accepted and agreed to the arrangements that had been made, and that in his opinion this was now no time, at this late hour, to start upsetting what had been agreed to and arranged with his, MacNeill's, full knowledge and consent. I remember he turned sharply and angrily to MacNeill, and said, 'It does not matter what you do or what you have done, the arrangements made will go ahead – we are determined that the manoeuvres as arranged will take place. We do not mind about your orders that went out today. The Volunteers of the country have a greater faith and trust and confidence in Pearse than they have in you.' He then used a phrase, to the exact words of which I cannot swear, 'The fight is on and it is up to you to decide now whether you are in it or not.' He turned angrily and left MacNeill and went away.

According to O'Kelly, MacNeill became very upset at this and asked him whether he thought it likely that the Volunteers would obey Pearse's orders rather than his. O'Kelly told him that he was certain that the Volunteers in Dublin, especially IRB members, would follow Pearse rather than MacNeill.

What concerned O'Kelly years later was something he had learned from MacNeill himself:

> I sat on there with MacNeill after he came back from the *Independent*. . . . It transpired during the course of that night in my talks with MacNeill that he had come to this decision about calling off the manouvres early on Saturday morning because he had sent out Ginger O'Connell, I am not sure where to, not later than Saturday morning to carry the countermanding order and to see that it was executed in different parts of South Leinster and Munster.

Surely this was the same Ginger O'Connell who, according to Min Ryan, was devastated when she had passed on the same message on Sunday!

Dr de Burca, who reported directly to Patrick Pearse and sometimes to Tom Clarke, and was living near Carrickmacross in County Monaghan 'immediately preceding the Rising', testifies that he:

> took the orders from Pearse to the Ulster Council on the Wednesday of Holy Week. I gave the orders to the Council collectively. . . . I returned to Dublin on the Thursday of Holy Week. There were . . . no orders for the Rising for any Ulster county except Belfast and Tyrone. The organisation elsewhere was scrappy. The majority of the men who travelled from Belfast to County Tyrone for the Rising were formerly Redmondite Volunteers who had much respect for Eoin MacNeill's orders. The Ulster Council of the IRB comprised five members. Denis McCullough and Dr Patrick MacCartain were members.

Nora Connolly O'Brien returned on Sunday morning from Belfast, in some disgust, because she had fully expected that action would take place there, and it had not. The Volunteers there had mobilised as they had been ordered, but after that nothing at all happened. She arrived at Liberty Hall to talk to her father before six o'clock in the morning. She wanted to know why the fight was off. The Volunteers had already gathered in Dungannon, and others were gathered in Coalisland. Connolly O'Brien thought there were about two hundred in total. At Coalisland, two young men delivered the message: they had received a demobilisation order, and there was to be no fighting. She had left for Dublin on the midnight train from Dungannon. What was happening? When she found her father, she remembers:

> He sat up in bed. The tears ran down his face. Evidently they had a meeting before that and he was very upset. Afterwards, I heard, they had a long session with MacNeill, and he [MacNeill] was absolutely obstinate about giving orders to go ahead: he would not. It must have been in conversation with my father that I got that information. We were so busy afterwards.

It would appear from Nora's evidence that it was Connolly who had called the long Sunday meeting, using his daughter and the girls who had come from Dungannon with her (six in all) to summon the key leaders to Liberty Hall. When she returned to Liberty Hall, Connolly was dressed in full uniform. It was the first time she had seen him in it:

> Daddy said, 'What about breakfast?' I agreed to get breakfast. I think Sean McDermott was the first to arrive, then Tom Clarke, and then Thomas MacDonagh; and after him I think it was Joseph Plunkett; I remember he was in his uniform, but his neck was all swathed in bandages; he was just getting over an operation; and Patrick Pearse was the last. I don't remember in what order Ceannt arrived but he was there too; he must have come between Plunkett and Pearse. I remember the order up to that. I remember Pearse came last. They sat down and had their breakfast.

7

'We Strike at Noon'

The long meeting began at about ten o'clock in the morning and lasted until 4 PM. All day long people came and went. Helena Molony, honorary secretary of Inghinidhe na hÉireann, remembers that Sunday as:

> a day of confusion, excitement and disappointment in Liberty Hall. I stayed there all day and all night. There was a lot of work to be done preparing food upstairs for the men who came from different parts of the city and had brought no rations. As a result of the calling-off of the fight, there was plenty of food. Large joints were cooked and all the [girls from the cooperative] were busy cutting up bread, butter and cooked meat.

It must have been a relief to find some work to do. Earlier, when they had seen MacNeill's countermanding order, they had all been heartbroken, and 'when they were not crying they were cursing,' Molony remembers.

Sean MacEntee arrived off the train looking for instructions. In his testimony, MacEntee dwells lovingly on every detail of his encounter with the nationalist leaders on this historic occasion. Pearse produced a revolver from a drawer and gave it to MacEntee, and Connolly fitted him out with some clothes. Suitably togged out and armed for all eventualities, MacEntee left Liberty Hall to catch the train for Ardee – only to miss it by a few minutes. One of the clocks on Liberty Hall was slow; that was the one that MacEntee had read. MacEntee's account of his return to Liberty Hall from the railway station to seek further help in this new situation makes painful reading. Sean McDermott in particular was furious. One has to admire MacEntee's courage in confessing to what had happened. It took him until 4 o'clock on Monday afternoon to rejoin his Volunteers, but he was able to relay the order from Pearse's own lips:

'Carry on the original instructions. We strike at noon.'

But that was not the end of MacEntee's difficulties. After he had reached his Volunteers, they had to get back to Dublin. They arrived in Dublin late on Wednesday morning. By then, he had been parted from the others for some hours. The journey had started auspiciously enough. They had boarded about fourteen cars and begun to drive through the night in the general direction of Dublin. They lost one another in the little roads round Tara, and one of the cars ran into a ditch. They lost Donal Hannigan, their leader. (Pearse appointed Hannigan Officer Commanding in Meath, Louth, south Down, south Armagh and Monaghan three weeks before the Rising, Sean Boylan reports in his statement.) When the petrol ran out at Dunshaughlin, MacEntee paid off the drivers of the hired cars and they proceeded on foot. Some of the party managed to get a lift on a passing cart and later joined up with Hannigan. But by this time, MacEntee had become exhausted and sat down to recover. He fell asleep or fainted – he did not know which – but when he awoke he was on his own. He pushed on painfully for Dublin. At Clonmeen, he hit the Finglas road – and had the good luck to meet a farmer called Dwyer, who was a friend of Eoin MacNeill and very obligingly drove in to Dublin on MacEntee's behalf:

> to find what the real position was. He was gone on this business rather longer than I expected, and it was almost three hours later when he returned. He told me that martial law had been proclaimed, and that he had learned from an English officer that Dublin was completely surrounded, that no German landings had taken place – the whole country round was alive with rumours of such landings – and

the bombardment of the Post Office would begin on the morrow. It was then considerably after seven o'clock and therefore impossible to make Dublin before dusk. I bade my friend goodbye and went back to the hay shed to spend the night.

Next morning, he managed to get into the city. After eating a good dinner in the kitchen of the Continental Café, which had been taken over by the Volunteers, he was assigned to military duties in the building adjoining Clery's on Earl Street.

The Louth volunteers were particularly unfortunate in the lead-up to the Rising. They had started off with a fairly respectable number and were on their way to Dublin when they received the countermanding order. The impact of MacNeill's order was more serious the further one was from Dublin because it was difficult for Volunteers to turn around and come back.

According to Tom Harris in County Kildare, on Easter Sunday, Lieutenant Ted O'Kelly, his superior officer in the Volunteers, was very upset when he read the countermanding order in the *Sunday Independent:*

> He said he had got the Sunday paper where MacNeill had issued the countermanding order. He did not attach any importance to MacNeill's order because he said he was not a member of the IRB.

MacNeill's dispatches stopping the Rising were circulating in the Curragh area. Harris and O'Kelly agreed that they had to find Tom Byrne, 'The Boer', an IRB man who had been sent to Ireland to lead them. They found him at Bodenstown. But at 4 o'clock in Naas, Harris recalls:

> Dick Stokes came along on a motorcycle, he recognised Byrne and O'Kelly, stopped and said he had a dispatch from Pearse that it was at 12 o'clock the next day the rising was to take place.

The object of the three – Ted O'Kelly, Tom Harris and Tom Byrne – then was to cover the whole area in order to tell their men

BACK TO NORMALITY The gutted GPO from upper Sackville Street (now O'Connell Street) after the Rising

(Desmond FitzGerald Photographs, UCDAD, P80/PH/2)

PRISONER UNDER ESCORT Mr James O'Connor, a member of St Margaret's Company of the Irish Volunteers, who took part in the 1916 action at Ashbourne, County Meath, pictured under escort en route to Richmond Barracks for eventual internment in Wakefield Prison, England

(Ref BMH WS 142. Courtesy of the Military Archives, Cathal Brugha Barracks, Rathmines, Dublin 6)

A group of Volunteers and one member of the Citizen Army (second from left) pictured inside the GPO, Dublin, Easter Week 1916
(Ref BMH WS 142. Courtesy of the Military Archives, Cathal Brugha Barracks, Rathmines, Dublin 6)

Two Volunteers pictured inside the GPO, Dublin, Easter Week 1916
(Ref BMH WS 142. Courtesy of the Military Archives, Cathal Brugha Barracks, Rathmines, Dublin 6)

FLYING THE FLAG The flag flown from the GPO by the insurgents during the Rising

(Courtesy Independent Newspapers Ireland)

THE AFTERMATH The GPO from O'Connell Bridge after the Rising
(Courtesy Independent Newspapers Ireland)

RICHARD MULCAHY Mulcahy was second-in-command to Thomas Ashe at the
Battle of Ashbourne and later head of the Free State forces
(Courtesy Independent Newspapers Ireland)

A Defining Moment
The clock from the
General Post Office

(Courtesy Independent
Newspapers Ireland)

Standing guard A soldier on
duty outside a ruined building,
possibly near the Munster and
Leinster Bank on Sackville Street

(Desmond FitzGerald Photographs,
UCDAD, P80/PH/3)

CLOSING IN British soldiers
in defensive position
crouched in the doorway of
a ruined building

(Desmond FitzGerald
Photographs, UCDAD,
P80/PH/9)

SCENE OF DEVASTATION
Extensive damage beside
the tram tracks at the junction of Carlisle Bridge
(now O'Connell Bridge)
and Westmoreland Street

(Desmond FitzGerald
Photographs, UCDAD,
P80/PH/6)

POBLACHT NA H EIREANN.

THE PROVISIONAL GOVERNMENT

OF THE

IRISH REPUBLIC

TO THE PEOPLE OF IRELAND.

IRISHMEN AND IRISHWOMEN: In the name of God and of the dead generations from which she receives her old tradition of nationhood, Ireland, through us, summons her children to her flag and strikes for her freedom.

Having organised and trained her manhood through her secret revolutionary organisation, the Irish Republican Brotherhood, and through her open military organisations, the Irish Volunteers and the Irish Citizen Army, having patiently perfected her discipline, having resolutely waited for the right moment to reveal itself, she now seizes that moment, and, supported by her exiled children in America and by gallant allies in Europe, but relying in the first on her own strength, she strikes in full confidence of victory.

We declare the right of the people of Ireland to the ownership of Ireland, and to the unfettered control of Irish destinies, to be sovereign and indefeasible. The long usurpation of that right by a foreign people and government has not extinguished the right, nor can it ever be extinguished except by the destruction of the Irish people. In every generation the Irish people have asserted their right to national freedom and sovereignty; six times during the past three hundred years they have asserted it in arms. Standing on that fundamental right and again asserting it in arms in the face of the world, we hereby proclaim the Irish Republic as a Sovereign Independent State, and we pledge our lives and the lives of our comrades-in-arms to the cause of its freedom, of its welfare, and of its exaltation among the nations.

The Irish Republic is entitled to, and hereby claims, the allegiance of every Irishman and Irishwoman. The Republic guarantees religious and civil liberty, equal rights and equal opportunities to all its citizens, and declares its resolve to pursue the happiness and prosperity of the whole nation and of all its parts, cherishing all the children of the nation equally, and oblivious of the differences carefully fostered by an alien government, which have divided a minority from the majority in the past.

Until our arms have brought the opportune moment for the establishment of a permanent National Government, representative of the whole people of Ireland and elected by the suffrages of all her men and women, the Provisional Government, hereby constituted, will administer the civil and military affairs of the Republic in trust for the people.

We place the cause of the Irish Republic under the protection of the Most High God, Whose blessing we invoke upon our arms, and we pray that no one who serves that cause will dishonour it by cowardice, inhumanity, or rapine. In this supreme hour the Irish nation must, by its valour and discipline and the readiness of its children to sacrifice themselves for the common good, prove itself worthy of the august destiny to which it is called.

Signed on Behalf of the Provisional Government,

THOMAS J. CLARKE,

SEAN Mac DIARMADA.   THOMAS MacDONAGH.
P. H. PEARSE,   EAMONN CEANNT,
JAMES CONNOLLY.   JOSEPH PLUNKETT.

THE PROCLAMATION OF THE IRISH REPUBLIC The document was read out by Patrick Pearse on the steps of the GPO on Easter Monday 1916

(Courtesy Independent Newspapers Ireland)

to be ready at 12 o'clock in Bodenstown. Between them, they covered the Athgarvan, Newbridge and Ballysax townlands in one part of the county, and Prosperous, Naas and Rathangan in another. They met that evening at the Prince of Wales Hotel in Newbridge. After tea, they remained talking and went to bed reasonably sure of a respectable turnout the next day. On the Monday morning, the first man they called on was in bed. He had no intention of turning out 'until the bungle of yesterday was set right,' he said.

All the three could do was to call on the Dominican College to collect some gelignite which had been left in the laboratory to be minded by one of the priests, Father McCluskey. Father McCluskey was sympathetic and was probably in the "know" of what was to happen. Harris recalls that 'The three of us started for Bodenstown – a Captain, a Lieutenant and a Private.'

But no one turned up in Bodenstown, so they dumped the explosives and went on to Maynooth to join up with the Maynooth Volunteers. They set out for Dublin marching sometimes along the railway and other times along the canal banks. They waded through the River Tolka to get to Glasnevin Cemetery.

The account given by Domhnall Ó Buachalla of the County Kildare action is remarkably consistent with Tom Harris's. Ó Buachalla, from Maynooth, had joined the Volunteers as soon as they had been set up. He did all the route marches and physical training that being a Volunteer entailed. Their company was small after the Redmondite split, but Ó Buachalla and the other Maynooth Volunteers doggedly continued to train and started firing practice with the very small number of rifles they could muster between them. Ó Buachalla recalls:

Some time before Easter Week 1916, I bought a service rifle (Lee-Enfield) in Keegan's Gun Shop on the Quays. I also bought some shotguns in Henshaw's. I got some ammunition for the service rifles at Keegan's and, all told, I managed to collect about two hundred rounds. We made buckshot for the sporting guns, about a couple of dozen rounds for each gun.

The Maynooth Volunteers never got round to electing officers, and no officers from Headquarters came to visit them. Domhnall Ó Buachalla never joined the IRB. Nobody told him that a Rising was planned for Easter. He continues:

> We received no orders or instructions prior to Easter Week.
> On Easter Monday afternoon I learned from a bread-van driver that fighting was taking place in Dublin between the Volunteers and the British military. I got on my [bicycle] and proceeded to Dublin to get instructions and find out what we were to do.

He got through to Dawson Street to the Headquarters of the Volunteers, only to find the place locked up. He had no choice but to return to Maynooth:

> I cycled through the Park and back to Maynooth. On reaching Maynooth I found Tom Byrne of Boer War fame, and Tom Harris there.

Byrne was put in command of the Maynooth detachment. Volunteer Jack Maguire was sent across to Dunboyne to contact Sean Boylan. He failed to show up. Byrne and his men marched off to the Rising. On their way, they called in to Maynooth College to ask the President of Maynooth, the Right Reverend John F. Hogan, for his blessing. The latter said he did not approve of what they were doing, but he blessed them anyway. The students were in a state of great excitement and cheered the Volunteers on their way. Ó Buachalla remembers:

> A servant boy in the College, who was not a Volunteer, joined us and came all the way to Dublin with us and fought there during the week.

The whole party, about eighteen men in all, arrived in Glasnevin Cemetery at about 2 or 3 AM. As soon as the cemetery opened, Byrne ventured out and found that the way into the city was open. Tom Harris describes what followed:

We took our guns and marched into the GPO. We did not meet anyone except a few Volunteer outposts around Blackquire Bridge, which passed us through. We got into the Post Office. Every place was quiet at that period. Numbers of people were on the street looking around. We had tea and eggs and cigars. I thought we should have got a rest. Connolly paraded us and said, 'it didn't matter a damn if we were wiped out now as we had justified ourselves.' I thought it a bit rugged.

The situation of the men in Meath was worse than that of the men in Kildare. At least the small band under the command of Tom Byrne got to the Rising. Not so Sean Boylan and his men in Dunboyne. Despite Boylan's earlier independent stance – he had held himself aloof from the local Irish Volunteers in 1914 – Boylan was appointed to look after the Meath area on the General Council of the Irish Volunteers. This council consisted of Eoin MacNeill (President), Pearse Plunkett, Thomas MacDonagh, Éamonn Ceannt, Sean McDermott, Bulmer Hobson and a representative from each county.

Despite his somewhat prominent position in the Volunteers and his membership of the IRB, Boylan did not have what might be called 'a good 1916'. He failed to turn up in Dunboyne to join the Maynooth Volunteers. The message from Tom Byrne, reinstating plans for the Rising, which Jack Maguire left for him, came too late. Boylan recalls:

On Good Friday evening I got written instructions from Pearse to the effect that the Rising would start at 6 PM on Easter Sunday. I do not remember who brought me this dispatch. Two men came with it and I remember I had to acknowledge it.

At about 4 PM on Easter Sunday evening a man called Benson arrived with a verbal message to say that the Rising was off. He stated that Sean Tobin of IRB Headquarters had sent him.

Boylan set about obeying this latest order immediately. He put an enormous amount of energy into stopping the mobilisation. He was away for what remained of Sunday and spent the night in Navan. When he heard on Monday that the Rising had started in the city after all, he found it almost impossible to mobilise his Volunteers again. Like many of the officers of the British army, the Volunteers had gone to the races at Fairyhouse.

In the end, Boylan did not make it to the Rising. A curious feature of his experience of the events of 1916 was that, at roughly the same time as he was receiving the countermanding order from IRB Headquarters, Dick Stokes, on his motorcycle in Naas, was delivering the message from Patrick Pearse ordering that the Rising go ahead – as indeed it did, at noon the following day.

The witness statement given by Claire Hobson, née Gregan, affords us a different perspective altogether on the events of 1916. She was not a member of the Volunteer movement but is nonetheless a unique witness. She worked at No. 2 Dawson Street. She was engaged to her boss, Bulmer Hobson, and knew most of the people connected with the revolutionary movement. She had good reason to remember the events of Easter weekend of 1916 from Good Friday to the end of the next week:

> I remember Bulmer telling me that he had to see MacNeill about preventing the Rising and he afterwards told me that he had seen him. It might have been Thursday he went but I can't definitely state that. It was probably on Good Friday he had been out to Woodtown.

Mrs Hobson could not remember how or when she heard that Bulmer had been 'arrested'. On either Friday or Saturday, she went to Padraig O'Riain's house in Clonliffe Road to make inquiries about him, accompanied by Sean Lester, a Belfast man and a Volunteer. They had no luck. Bulmer Hobson had in fact been detained in the home of Martin Conlon, another IRB man; this fact is confirmed in Conlon's statement as well as in that of Maurice Collins. The latter tells us that, instead of parading on the Sunday, he and his company assembled in North Frederick Street to await the outcome of a meeting at IRB Headquarters:

> Word reached us that the Rising was to take place at 12 o'clock on Easter Monday. In the meantime I was instructed to proceed with my rifle to Martin Conlon's house, Cabra Park, to take charge of Bulmer Hobson, who was detained there as a prisoner. Michael Lynch of 'F' Company was also with me. We found Hobson in a rather distressed state of mind, and had to warn him several times to remain calm and quiet. . . . While he was a prisoner with us, his fiancée called, inquiring if Bulmer Hobson were there, but we considered it better to deny his presence. We held him prisoner until Wednesday night when an order came, signed by Pearse or Connolly, that Hobson could be released.

But on Sunday Claire Hobson did not know that. She went to Liberty Hall. When she asked to see James Connolly, she was told that there was an important conference on. Eventually, however, she saw Connolly, and later Pearse. They agreed with her that Bulmer was a perfectly honest man but said that he had to be held prisoner lest he interfere with the plans for a rising. She also saw Sean McDermott. Claire did not like McDermott; nor, it appears, did Bulmer. Claire Hobson relates that:

> He [Bulmer] thought him slippery, that he would seem to side with Bulmer's point of view while eventually he proved he was going in another direction. Sean always struck me as deadly sly. I also felt that a long life did not interest him much as he was not a strong man and was due for another operation.

Claire continued to search for Bulmer's whereabouts. She went into the city just after the Rising had begun. The Volunteers had occupied the GPO and it seemed at that stage that all options were still open to the members of the revolutionary movement. She met Sean Lester near Trinity College. He told her that he wished he could see and talk to Bulmer. Claire Hobson continues:

I then asked him was he going into the Rising. He seemed uncertain but he thought he would, though he really believed that Bulmer and those on the committee who thought like him were right.

Claire Hobson was admitted into the GPO with no great difficulty when she said she wanted to see Patrick Pearse. She was able to talk to, amongst others, Desmond FitzGerald, whom she encountered as she was taking leave of Pearse:

> Just then Desmond FitzGerald came out of a room and greeted me affectionately, calling out, 'Hello, Claire'. He was very cheerful. I asked him, 'What are you doing?' What he answered was, 'I am looking after the girls.' He asked me would I have a cup of tea. I said 'No, thank you', adding that I was looking for Sean Lester.

When the IRB eventually released Bulmer Hobson, he sent word of what had happened. Claire Gregan remembered receiving the message on Tuesday. Maurice Collins believed that the order to release Hobson came on Wednesday. But according to Martin Conlon's testimony, the order arrived on Monday:

> Such orders did in fact arrive in the course of the afternoon of Easter Monday. They were brought by Mr Sean T. O'Kelly . . . By then I was no longer in the house, having 'mobilised' for the Rising and taken up my post in Church Street with my Volunteer Unit. The orders, which President O'Kelly brought, were in writing and came from Sean McDermott.

Bulmer Hobson and Claire Gregan went out to Woodtown Park in Dundrum, the home of James MacNeill, Eoin MacNeill's brother. Eoin MacNeill was not there. Claire was told that he had gone to see the Augustinians in Orlagh. Perhaps we can deduce from this testimony that Bulmer Hobson was not the only influence on Eoin MacNeill's life, and certainly not the strongest. Who would need advice more than MacNeill at this desperate juncture of his life, and who was more qualified to give it than some now-unknown Augustinian?

The young couple, Bulmer Hobson and Clare Gregan, stayed at Woodtown until their marriage later in the year.

8

MEN AND WOMEN OF THE CITIZEN ARMY

According to Frank Robbins, whose testimony on the matter is referred to in Chapter Five, when Michael Mallin met the Military Council at the time of Connolly's disappearance, Éamonn Ceannt was very sarcastic about the Citizen Army. Mallin was deeply hurt. It seems that Mallin, in his determination to have Connolly released forthwith, was somewhat provocative. According to Robbins, Mallin said:

> 'In case you may think of arresting me as you have arrest-
> ed Connolly, I want to tell you that that will not have any
> effect on the situation. There will be no more talking or
> interviews. There will be action.' Éamonn Ceannt, who was
> sitting near Mallin, asked in a sarcastic tone, 'And what
> could your small number do in such a situation?'. Mallin
> replied, 'We can fight and die, and it will be to our glory and
> your shame if such takes place.' With that, Patrick Pearse
> banged the table, saying, 'Yea, by God, that is so, and here's
> one who will be with you.'

It is easy to understand Mallin's hurt. The Citizen Army had much to be proud of. They might not have had the numbers of the Volunteers but they had cohesion and discipline, both of which should have been emulated by any body that was seriously thinking of armed rebellion.

Around the time of the 1913 Lockout, Connolly had announced his intention of organising and disciplining a force to protect workers' meetings 'and to prevent the brutalities of armed thugs occurring in the future.' It is scarcely surprising that a former British army man, such as Connolly was, would see the advantages that such a force would offer in the event of the kind of street rioting which marked the struggle for social justice in early-twentieth-century Dublin. Michael Mallin, next in command to Connolly , was also ex-British army, and had served in India. (In the Ireland of that time, the British army was an important source of employment, and membership in it did not necessarily indicate any ideological bent.)

Connolly had worked for the labour movemernt since the early 1900s. From 1902 until 1909, he had been an organiser for the same movement, training in his daughter, Nora, in the same line of work. As Mallin recalls:

> Later, he was working with the Transport Union; and he went up to Belfast as their Northern representative. He had the docks mainly, and he did really very well for the dock workers. They had terrific, ferocious conditions. He got all that changed. Then the mill girls – their fathers, brothers and uncles were working in the docks – went on strike, although they were not organised.

Nora was at once put to work with them. Later she joined the only girls' branch of the Fianna in Ireland. When they expanded their activities and founded a political party, with the boys, called the Irish Republican Party, they attracted the notice of Patrick Pearse, who praised their enthusiasm in his publication *An Claidheamh Soluis*. In the winter they met at the Belfast Freedom Club, which was owned by the IRB.

Not everyone in the revolutionary movement liked the Irish Volunteers. Survivors of the 1913 Lockout found it hard to associate with people who were suspected of having sided against the workers in that epic struggle. For example, Joseph Scollan, the leader of the Hibernian Rifles, kept himself somewhat aloof from the main body of the Volunteers. The Redmond split did not affect the Hibernian Rifles. More importantly, neither did MacNeill's countermand. They continued to drill, march and buy as many rifles as they could from badly paid British soldiers:

At the time of O'Donovan Rossa's funeral the Hibernian Rifles paraded one hundred and fifty strong with fifty rifles. Connolly and I were in close association and through him I understood it was intended to have an insurrection but I had no idea of when it would take place. There were no overtures to me by any of the leaders of the Irish Volunteers to co-operate with them.

From the very first time he had heard Connolly mention the idea of a Citizen Army, Frank Robbins could hardly wait to join, but the next mention of an army was made by James Larkin. Larkin stipulated that this new army should be made up of men who were at least six foot tall. Neither did he want boys – only 'fully grown' men. Robbins would not qualify on either count: he was quite short and did not look fully grown. After the Howth gun-running, he almost joined the Volunteers. At last, however, he presented himself timidly at Liberty Hall:

> To my great joy, the three men who were seated around the table – Messrs Braithwaite, Seamus MacGowan and Sean O'Casey – told me that it was young men like myself they were seeking.

But the really outstanding Citizen Army people were the women. That extraordinary group, who had begun their political life long before the Citizen Army started to recruit, felt very much at home with James Connolly and his men. Dr Kathleen Lynn, Helena Molony, Rosanna Hackett, Madeline ffrench-Mullan and Margaret Skinneder were amongst those who, as well as rolling bandages, transporting arms and ammunition, and tending the wounded, fought side by side with the men. Helena Molony, who was Secretary of Inghinidhe na hÉireann from 1907 to 1914, was involved in the foundation of a remarkable journal for women called *Bean na hÉireann,* which owed its existence partly to an effort to counteract the influence of Arthur Griffith's Sinn Féin, with its emphasis on passive resistance. In her testimony, Molony sets out their point of view:

We could not see any virtue in joining a mere Repeal Movement. The original object of Sinn Féin was to restore the Irish Parliament of 1782. We considered that the ideals of Tone, Davis, [John] Mitchel, and Fintan Lalor were being pushed into the bachground.

Moreover, she and her friends did not like Sinn Féin's ideas on how society should be organised:

The social ideals of Sinn Féin did not appeal to us. They wished to see Irish society (as their official organ once expressed it) 'a progressive and enlightened aristocracy, a prosperous middle class, and a happy and contented working class'. It all sounded dull, and a little bit vulgar to us.

These women were intensely conscious of their status as revolutionaries.

Years later, in a letter to the writer Sean O'Faolain, Helena Molony spoke for them all. The letter, dated 6 September 1934, deals with the biography of Countess Markievicz, in which Molony had had some part:

It is a curious thing that many men seem to be unable to believe that any woman can embrace an ideal – accept it intellectually, feel it as a profound emotion, and then calmly decide to make a vocation of working for its realisation – they give themselves endless pains to prove that every serious thing a woman does (outside nursing babies or washing pots) is the result of being in love with some man, or disappointment in love of some man, or looking for excitement, or limelight, or indulging their vanity. You do not seem to have escaped from the limitations of your sex, therefore you describe Madame as being 'caught up' by or rallying 'to the side of' Connolly, Larkin, or some man or other, whereas the simple fact is that she was working, as a man might have worked, for the freedom of Ireland. She [Markievicz] allied herself with these later movements because they were advancing the ideals which she had accepted years before. We were writing about Labour conditions – woman's labour in particular – years before Larkin came to Ireland, and she never 'abandoned' or 'drew away from' that cause.

It is unlikely that Helena Molony, Madam Markievicz or any of the other women had any problems with James Connolly's attitude to gender. He was a remarkable man: he was, among other things, a true feminist.

The Citizen Army had emerged from the searing experience of the Dublin workers in the 1913 Lockout and the events that had led up to it. It gave their army a unity and purpose which was proof against the disappointment of MacNeill's countermanding order. Molony had one thought:

'I can't believe this will really happen. I know we can depend on the Citizen Army, but what about the rest?'

The Citizen Army would fight on their own even if all others abandoned the Rising.

In his witness statement, Frank Robbins provides an index at the beginning of the document, which details the main features and events in the history of the Citizen Army. The preparations for the insurrection were meticulous.

James Larkin left for America in 1914 and James Connolly was brought to Dublin in October. Connolly threw himself into the work of the Citizen Army. At the same time, he had to keep the bankrupt ITGWU alive. His Chief of Staff was Michael Mallin, who, as soon as he had been appointed, added outdoor exercises to the work of the Citizen Army. Almost every Sunday and Bank Holiday was spent in this way. Quite frequently, they met Con Colbert of the Volunteers; the Citizen Army sometimes engaged in exercises with the Volunteers. Another means of training used by Connolly and Mallin was the carrying out of mock attacks on various buildings in the city. Frank Robbins remembers:

One night in particular, late in 1915, a mock attack was arranged for Dublin Castle. One would have imagined that the powers above were friendly to us because on that night we were favoured with a thick heavy fog over Dublin.

Complete mobilisation of the Citizen Army had been ordered. All paraded at Liberty Hall, and various companies and sections were detailed from there to go in different directions. Each officer had his separate instructions, known only to himself, in each Section or Company as to the route he was to take and the time he was to take and the time he was to arrive at the final point. Our Company arrived at Ship Street on the stroke of midnight, and as we marched in, other Sections were also marching in from various other points. The tramping of feet from the different directions was slightly startling and some of us wondered was this the hour we had all been looking forward to.

Connolly and Mallin were pleased with the success of the exercise. But the night was not over. They all marched to Emmet Hall, the branch offices of the ITGWU in Inchicore. The women's section of the Army had refreshments ready and the party lasted until the early hours of Sunday morning. The party was made all the more enjoyable by the fact that the Dublin Metropolitan Police (who had followed as many of the men as they could since they started out) 'kept their vigil all through the night out in the cold.'

The Citizen Army was fond of concerts, as indeed were the Volunteers. Frank Robbins lists the names of those who sang at these concerts. Robbins himself had a fine voice; later in his life, when he was in the United States, he was offered the chance of becoming a professional singer. Michael Mallin also organised a small orchestra.

James Connolly regularly gave lectures on street fighting to his men. Shortly before the Rising, Robbins learned that Connolly had been giving these lectures to Volunteer officers as well. The lectures were greatly appreciated. Connolly emphasised the essential points of street-fighting, such as maintaining the water supply for human use and as a protection against fire; never to occupy a corner building without proper support from each side; the necessity for breaching walls so that a whole street of any length could be occupied. At the end of these lectures, when Connolly invited questions as to ways and means, the necessity of procuring equipment that was useful in this kind of battle action became apparent.

109

Unfortunately, the Citizen Army lacked the means to buy the equipment. To any man working in the Dublin Dockyard, however, the solution was obvious: they could steal them. Sledgehammers were supplied by the Company; the type most favoured were the seven-pound ones. Robbins notes that 'Other articles among the many which the Dublin Dockyard Company lost from time to time were files, pieces of lathes, and borings, the latter being used in the preparation of home-made bombs.'

As the Volunteers spread all over the country, many of the Feiseanna ran competitions for the best-drilled Company. The Irish Citizen Army entered a number of events. Going to these events involved exciting train journeys to places like Tullow in County Carlow. But mostly they took place on the outskirts of Dublin, at places such as St Enda's and Father Matthew Park in Fairview. The Citizen Army did well in these competitions; Frank Robbins gives all the credit for their achievements in the competitions to their drill instructors, who had all been attached to the British army in their younger days. Like Michael Mallin, one of them, John O'Neill, had served in India. He was very keen on Morse code and persuaded some young people to study it. Two others had fought in the Boer War. They all went on to fight in Easter Week, where, according to Frank Robbins, they 'proved themselves to be very fine officers.'

For some weeks before the Rising, Liberty Hall became less a trade-union headquarters than an army barracks. Frank Robbins was amongst those who took up residence there, going home only at weekends, for a change of clothing. He, like the others, spent most of his time making munitions. Every so often, Connolly, Mallin or Madame Markievicz dropped in to see them. Madam Markievicz almost always brought a bag of cakes for their tea. On one of her afternoon visits, Robbins recalled her saying: 'I have already overdrawn my bank account for my next quarter's allowance to the extent of £45, and if this bally revolution doesn't take place soon I don't know how I'm going to live.'

Connolly and the Citizen Army used the last few days before the Rising to mark his appreciation of Dr Kathleen Lynn's help with medical preparations for the Rising. On Holy Thursday, they presented her with a present of a gold brooch. Dr Lynn recalls:

> It was a gold brooch in the form of a fibula and it is still my most treasured possession.

Michael Mallin had also composed a poem for the occasion, but Dr Lynn had lost that.

Helena Molony remembered Liberty Hall in these last weeks as being a place of intense activity, particularly at weekends:

> Every Saturday and Sunday the men would be there all day. Dinner would be served for them. The Citizen Army was a very unmilitary-looking body of men; very free and easy from a military point of view. Those who could not go home would have their meals there. They had two big halls where they stacked their arms. Some of them kept their arms at home.

The women too were kept very busy:

> For the last fortnight before Easter, Jinny Shanahan and I were actually sleeping at night on a pile of men's coats in the back of the shop. I had all my clothes there, including my spare underclothing, with the result that when I was arrested on Easter Monday at the City Hall I had not a thing to change into, and had to borrow from Nell Ryan and Dr Lynn, who were in prison too.

The scene and the atmosphere in Liberty Hall during the few days before the Rising in Dublin in 1916 were probably very similar to those found in any of the other European cities where men and women prepared for revolution at various points in the nineteenth and early twentieth centuries. Michael Mallin added a detail that only he could have contributed. Again, Robbins remembers:

> A few days before the insurrection Commandant Mallin brought in to our workroom a weaving loom and he, in his spare time, came in for the purpose of weaving some poplin. He told me he hoped to get the piece finished

before the insurrection, and if this were accomplished he would get the sum of £10 for it. This money he proposed giving to Mrs Mallin to help tide her over the awkward period while the fighting was taking place in the city.

Michael Mallin was one of those executed after the Rising.

9

Occupying the Buildings

No one could say that either of those two wonderful female members of the Citizen Army, Helena Molony and Dr Kathleen Lynn, enjoyed the fighting involved in the 1916 Rising. Countess Markievicz did not make a witness statement, so we do not have her first-hand account. Helena Molony remembered what she herself wore on the day of the Rising:

> I has an Irish tweed costume, with a Sam Browne belt. I had my own revolver and ammunition. At the last minute when we were going off at twelve o'clock, Connolly gave out revolvers to our girls, saying: 'Don't use them except as a last resort.'
>
> There were nine girls in our party, going to the Castle.

Dublin Castle was chosen as an early target because of its psychological significance. It had been, as Molony put it, 'the citadel of foreign rule for seven hundred years.'

Molony was not the only witness who remarked, thirty years later, on the degree of vagueness and imprecision that existed regarding what the members of the Citizen Army were to do up to the last minute before engagement:

> I did not know beforehand what was to take place. I did not know to which place I was going. I remember being rather surprised at not going to the GPO with James Connolly. Winnie Carney acted as his secretary all through. She was a very good shorthand typist. I remember I wondered at his

saying to me: 'You go with Sean.' As I said already, Sean was an old friend, and acted in the Abbey Theatre along with me.

Molony describes the short journey from Liberty Hall, up Dame Street to the Castle. On Connolly's orders, they moved in detachments, with Sean Connolly leading the men; the nine women, with Helena Molony at their head:

> simply followed the men. Sean turned left and went towards the Castle Gate. I think there may have been other detachments behind us.

Helena Molony vividly remembered what happened next:

> It was at the Castle the first shot was fired. . . . I, with my girls, followed Sean Connolly and his party. We went right up to the Castle Gate, up the narrow street. Just then, a police sergeant came out and, seeing our determination, he thought it was a parade, and that it probably would be going up Ship Street. When Connolly went to go past him, the sergeant put out his arm; and Connolly shot him dead. When the military guard saw that it was serious, he pulled the gates to.

The men following Connolly were meant to push their way through, but whether because of hesitation, or because they had not been properly prepared, or because of the shooting of the policeman, they lost that opportunity. Molony recalls: 'On the flash, the gates were closed.'

She believed that 'guarded secrecy, not to let it look like anything other than the manoeuvres which were taking place for weeks before, may have been the reason; but certainly there was hesitation.'

In any case, they did not get in; many years later, the bitter disappointment about this fact surfaced in Molony's testimony. The Citizen Army might have captured the Undersecretary, who was having lunch at the Castle. Molony's narrative returns to the dead policeman:

Connolly said in an excited voice, 'Get in, get in.' He was excited because he shot the policeman dead. We were all in excitement. When I saw Connolly draw his revolver, I drew my own. Across the road, there was a policeman with papers. He got away, thank God. I did not like to think of the policeman dead. I think there were a couple of soldiers killed later. I think the policeman at the gate was killed instantly.

The small contingent switched their attention to City Hall. They met with no opposition because it was a Bank Holiday.

The night before, Easter Sunday night, Dr Kathleen Lynn had stayed overnight at Mrs Wyse-Power's. She did not sleep very soundly. She recalls:

We knew well a rising was coming. . . . When I came along on Monday morning we were given our orders – typed out – where we were to go. They were signed by Mallin. . . . My assignment was the City Hall. Mme Markievicz and I were driven in my car from Liberty Hall by [name not given], who was a most reckless driver. Years later, in 1926, when Miss ffrench-Mullen and I were in New York, a car suddenly stopped in the street; he flung himself out of it and rushed out of it and rushed over to greet us.

The car dropped me and all my medical traps at the City Hall and I did not see it again for months. The idea was that Madame would use it going around to inspect the different posts; but when she got to Stephen's Green she stayed there with Mallin.

Sometime before noon, Dr Lynn got to City Hall, where Sean Connolly was already in occupation with his section of the Citizen Army. Sean Connolly suggested that some of them should go up on the roof. Dr Lynn continues:

It was a beautiful day, the sun was hot and we were not long there when we noticed Sean Connolly coming towards us, walking upright, although we had been advised to crouch and take cover as much as possible. We suddenly saw him fall mortally wounded by a sniper's bullet from the Castle. First aid was useless. He died almost immediately.

Helena Molony went into more detail:

I said an Act of Contrition into his ear. We had no priest. We were very distressed at Sean Connolly's death, I particularly, as I had known him for so long and acted with him. His young brother, Matt, who was only fifteen, was also on the roof and cried bitterly when he saw his brother dying.

Sean Connolly was the first member of the Citizen Army to lose his life in the Rising.

The plan for the Rising was fairly simple in outline. The rebels would seize important buildings in the centre of the city. They would defend these by occupying an outer ring of defendable buildings. The Volunteers were divided into four battalions. The 1st Battalion, commanded by Edward Daly (brother-in-law of Tom Clarke), was to assemble in Church Street; they were associated with the Four Courts. The 2nd Battalion was under the command of Thomas MacDonagh. They gathered in St Stephen's Green before taking over the Jacob's factory in Bishop Street. The 3rd Battalion seized Bolands Mills and some points on the route to Dun Laoghaire. Éamon de Valera – the only battalion commandant who was not executed after the Rising had been put down – headed this battalion. The 4th Battalion was under the command of Éamonn Ceannt; their headquarters was the South Dublin Union, now St James's Hospital.

In addition to these 'formal' arrangements, there were groups like the Kimmage Garrison, the men from Kildare and even individuals like Sean MacEntee, and Desmond FitzGerald and his wife Mabel, who made their own difficult way to the Rising. A small detachment, under Commandant Thomas Ashe and Vice

Commandant Richard Mulcahy, waited at the ready, on the borders of Dublin and Meath.

Like all the other witnesses, Seamus Robinson remembered his dismay on Easter Sunday morning, when he saw MacNeill's order countermanding the mobilisation. The men in Kimmage had guessed that the 'mobilisation' referred to was the rising for which they had been preparing for weeks. They had begun to discuss amongst themselves what action might be taken against those who were responsible for the cancellation of the mobilisation, when they discovered that the Rising was on again. Robinson recalls:

> On Easter Monday morning George Plunkett's preoccupied demeanour had changed. He was wearing a broad, proud, confident smile and a sword! Plunkett ordered us to parade with full equipment and hard rations. We assembled in the grounds, and about 11.15, without any indication to us rank-and-filers that the time for action had come, we were marched to the Dolphin's Barn tram terminus and boarded a tram for the city. We were, as far as I can recollect, about sixty strong. We left the tram at College Green and marched to Liberty Hall.

Beresford Place was full of Citizen Army men and women. Everything was bustle and excitement:

> Margaret Skinneder, whom I knew, rushed over to me and said 'It's on.' I asked 'What's on?' She said, 'The rebellion of course.' This was the first positive information I had that action was to be taken that morning.

After about twenty minutes, they were ordered to move up the quays and Robinson was put in charge of a section. A Volunteer called Peadar Bracken showed him an order from James Connolly indicating that they were to take over the two shops on the bridge, the jewellers' Hopkins and Hopkins, and Kelly's. Robinson continues:

Bracken said he would take over Kelly's and I was to take over Hopkins. Near the bridge I fell out of the ranks. . . . I was ipso facto made into a Lieutenant in charge of half of Bracken's Company!

The Garrison had been formed that morning ad hoc, as far as I ever knew, into two Companies. I was not then aware of this arrangement, neither was the rest of 'my' half-Company apparently, and so only a section followed me when I fell out of the ranks at the bridge. I had been marching in front all the way from Liberty Hall, and, not having any responsibility till the last exciting moment, I have no idea who the men were behind me in the Section or the Company.

The result was that Seamus Robinson had only four men, including himself, to take and hold Hopkins and Hopkins. Nonetheless, he managed to get into the premises and found two of his men already there. He was even able to persuade the garrison in the GPO to send some men to help. They sent three Citizen Army men. One of the three had a service rifle – the only man of the five who had one. They had shotguns and small arms and of course 'a fair supply of home-made grenades,' Robinson reports.

Robinson describes a strange episode in the exchange of gunfire with the British:

On Tuesday morning there was some shooting in our vicinity and we came to the conclusion that it was coming from McBirney's. I noticed that at one of the windows in McBirney's the figure of a girl, or what appeared to be a girl, used appear for a few moments and then go. Always after her appearance some shooting was heard and I concluded that she was either spotting for the gunner or was 'herself' doing the shooting. On one occasion after her disappearance I fired at the window where she had been. She did not appear any more.

This account is repeated almost exactly by Domhnall Ó Buachalla in his account of the day:

That evening (Tuesday) another man, whom I do not know, and I were detailed to proceed to the glass turret or dome of Arnott's in Henry Street. This was to try and keep sniping by the enemy from Westmoreland Street under control. I was given good field glasses. We used bales of cloth to barricade the dome and try and make it bullet-proof. There was sniping from Westmoreland Street direction, but it was impossible to locate the snipers. After some time I noticed that one of the upper windows of McBirney's drapery establishment on Aston Quay was opened, the rest being closed. I could see a waitress in her uniform carrying a tray past the window. It occurred to me that it was strange for a waitress to be on duty when the premises were closed, being right in the centre of the area where fighting was taking place. I got my glasses on to the window and, as I suspected, I observed a soldier in a stooped position in the far side of the room and holding a rifle. I took aim at the window and fired. The first shot was high, hitting over the window. My second shot went thro' the top pane and my third also went into the room. I did not see the waitress any more after this. No firing took place from that window afterwards.

Domhnall Ó Buachalla would appear to have been a useful marksman and after his time in Arnott's dome he was sent to deal with some sniping from the roof of Trinity College. On that same morning, nine men from the Maynooth group and eighteen men from the Hibernian Rifles were ordered to get over from the GPO to the Exchange Hotel soon after the Kildare men had arrived and been fed there. Tom Harris remembers:

We went down Liffey Street out on the Quays and across the Halfpenny Bridge. The toll man demanded a halfpenny. We got into the Exchange Hotel by the back door.

His account is less detailed than that of Domhnall Ó Buachalla. Joseph Scollan's testimony appears to be the clearest of the three:

We got into the Exchange Hotel and on to the roof. At this time some of the Volunteers were supposed to be trapped in the *Evening Mail* office and in the City Hall. We found that the British occupied the City Hall and we engaged them by fire. In the afternoon units of the Irish Fusiliers and Inniskilling Fusiliers advanced to storm our position and were met by a fusillade from our shotgun men and rifles. They were actually slaughtered by our fire. Twenty-three or [twenty]-four of them were killed or seriously wounded.

The men from Kildare and the men from Joseph Scollan's Hibernian Rifles held their position until about 4.30 that afternoon, when they were ordered back to the GPO.

At least the men from Kildare and Joseph Scollan's group had successfully carried out their orders. People like Sean Murphy, who had become a member of the IRB in 1901, had to endure extraordinary uncertainty in the last few hours before the Rising, because of, as he called it, 'the unfortunate publication of the Proclamation over the signature of Eoin MacNeill, who was undoubtedly inspired by [Bulmer] Hobson.'

Sean Murphy was extremely conscious of his responsibilities to the members of his Circle in the IRB and to a lesser extent to his company of Volunteers. He felt that he had to find out what was going to happen, 'knowing that there would be serious repercussions particularly amongst IRB members.' Twice he went to Sean Tobin's house in Hardwicke Street, where the Military Council was supposed to be meeting. He recalls:

I did not see Tobin on my second visit to his house. I saw Tom Clarke and also a man named Greg Murphy. He [Murphy] was a member of the Dublin Centres Board and was looked upon as a trusted messenger.

But no message came. Murphy concluded that the Rising was off and decided to try to save his job (possibly as a delivery man), which he was now in grave danger of losing. He went to Bray, where he spent some hours working. He cut his day's work short and returned to Dublin, only to hear that the insurrection had started and 'that the Volunteers were out all over the city.'

Murphy returned home to see if his wife knew anything about the Rising. She had heard nothing, but two members of his Company were waiting for him, to look for directions. While he was putting on his uniform, another 'lapsed' IRB member arrived asking to be allowed to join in whatever was going to happen. Murphy began the search for his company, sending a man called McDonnell to look for them. At last he found Thomas Hunter, another member of the IRB in command. It was no simple matter for them to join Thomas Hunter. Before Murphy could leave, he had to deal with that element of Dublin society which took a completely different view of the events of the time:

> On account of the hostile element round the house, my wife was nervous of remaining there, as previous to my return home part of the mob outside was trying to burn her out.

He helped to move her and their children to her mother's house in a street off Clanbrassil Street. He locked up, and brought his three men to Thomas Hunter. Murphy's first orders from Hunter were to go to the junction of Kevin Street and Patrick Street and hold it until Hunter got orders from his commandant in Jacob's factory. Only a short time before, according to Murphy, as told to him by Hunter:

> Some civilians had been very aggressive towards our men and . . . had attacked one of the Volunteers and in order to save his life they had to shoot one of the civilians.

That night Thomas MacDonagh ordered Hunter to fall back to Jacob's. Sean Murphy took up his position on the top of the building. In his witness statement, he recalls that:

> A series of windows overlooked the Adelaide Hospital and were in view of the Tower in the Castle, from where we

121

were under fire on the Wednesday by machine-guns. No casualties occurred among the men under my charge.

The Volunteers held Jacob's factory until the surrender on Sunday morning. On Wednesday night, a group of Volunteers on bicycles was sent to attack the troops around Clanwilliam House. One Volunteer was killed. Murphy states that they remained in their position 'through Thursday, Friday and Saturday, being sniped at occasionally from the Castle.'

10

'ALL IN GOOD SPIRITS'

When Robert Holland, from Inchicore in Dublin, gave his testimony to the Bureau of Military History in 1949, he was in his early fifties. His nineteenth birthday fell on the second day of the Rising. He writes:

> I must have slept a little through the night although I do not remember. On the following morning [Tuesday], which broke fine and sunny, I was nineteen years of age on that day, 25th April. My brother, Dan, came up to wish me a happy birthday and we wondered what part my father and my brothers, Walter and Frank, were playing [in the Rising] and where they were.

Holland appears to have been weaned on the republican movement. When he was twelve, he attended the very first meeting of Fianna Éireann, which took place in Brunswick Street in Dublin. There were about twenty-five people present at the meeting, which was addressed by Countess Markievicz. The Countess explained that she and the other adults there wished to establish the Fianna to act as a counterweight to Robert Baden-Powell's Boy Scouts. She held the view that the purpose of the Boy Scouts in Ireland was to prepare the youth of the country for joining the British army. Soon afterwards, Robert joined the Fianna. His first political outing was when the Fianna arranged a visit to Bodenstown on the occasion of King George V's arrival in Dublin in 1911. As a member of the Fianna, he took part in the Howth gun-running; he was able to procure a gun for himself during that episode.

There was a natural progression from the Fianna to membership of the Irish Volunteers; Robert joined the Volunteers at the age of around seventeen, when a branch was started in Inchicore. In 1915, he was invited to join the IRB. A man called Christy Byrne, a fitter's helper in Dublin Corporation, swore him into the Brotherhood. Holland remembers:

> I was told to attend a meeting of the IRB on the following Sunday at 12 o'clock in 41 Parnell Square. When I got there, there were about 20 to 30 men, all of whom seemed older than me, and I was surprised to see an older brother of mine there, Dan Holland. He said to me, 'You seem surprised, but you needn't be because Frank (another brother of mine) and my father are members of another Circle.'

Shortly after his induction into the IRB, Holland was singled out for special training. Con Colbert, who was his immediate superior and one of those executed after the Rising, wanted him:

> to go whole-time with him in the Irish Volunteers. I was sent to two special classes in No. 2 Dawson Street, one was for lectures in street fighting and the other was lectures on first aid. That took up the whole winter of 1915 and the early months of 1916.

The Holland home at 157 Inchicore Road was very useful in the weeks preceding the Rising. Just five weeks before Easter, the family was able to store seven cases of American .22 rifles for the Volunteers. Robert and his company were very busy. Like Joseph Scollan, they set about equipping themselves. Holland remembers:

> A spurt was put on to encourage the men to get their hands on service rifles and .305 ammunition. These could be bought from British soldiers who were returning on leave from France and other war zones. Prices ranged from £5 to £7 per rifle, and if a soldier was drunk enough we relieved him of his rifle without compensation.

As Easter drew near, it was clear that the Holland family need-
ed to talk. They left it until Holy Saturday evening, when Tom
Young, another Volunteer, came to the house with orders for
Robert. The latter was told to mobilise and to bring:

> forty-eight hours' ration . . . The mobilisation was for
> Sunday at 10 o'clock at Emerald Square, Dolphin's Barn.
> When my father came home on Saturday night, he, my
> brothers Frank, Dan, and Walter, and myself had a family
> meeting. Frank, who was my eldest brother, made his deci-
> sion that the four sons would go out if my father stayed at
> home. Frank had already posted us and he pointed out that
> my mother was a cripple and we had a young sister then
> about seven years of age. My father kicked up a row about
> this decision and said he had spent all his life both in the
> Fenians and in the IRB and that *he* would go out whether *we*
> went out or not. We could not persuade him to stay at home
> and left it at that.

This reaction from the older generation was not unique.
Seamus Dobbyn from Belfast, a member of the Supreme Council
of the IRB, had much the same experience with his father, except
that Mr Dobbyn did not discuss the matter with his son but simply
turned up in Dungannon.

The confusion caused by Eoin MacNeill's countermand was
dealt with in F Company 4th Battalion under Con Colbert. At six
o'clock on Easter Sunday morning, Colbert called to Robert
Holland's house with new orders, and Holland spent all Easter
Sunday contacting his men. Nobody was to go far from home without leaving word as to where they were to be found. Holland did
not finish until 6 o'clock that evening. He went to bed at 10.30 PM,
after attending 'the usual Sunday night *ceilidhe*' in Donore Avenue.

That morning he got up at 7 o'clock and began mobilising for
the real rising. He arrived at Emerald Square at 10 AM in good time.
'There were then about a hundred Volunteers in the Square with
Éamonn Ceannt in charge,' he recalls.

Holland was told of the positions that the 4th Battalion would
take up: Con Colbert was to occupy Ardee Street Brewery, Seamus

Murphy was to take Marrowbone Lane Distillery, the Headquarters would be in the South Dublin Union, with Éamonn Ceannt in charge, and Captain Tommy McCarthy was to occupy Roe's Distillery at Mount Brown.

When Holland was leaving the Square sometime later, dressed in mufti, with knickerbockers, long stockings and leggings, about a hundred and fifty men and fifty members of Cumann na mBan had assembled. He arrived at Ardee Street Brewery at 12 o'clock but found the gates locked, 'with a very rowdy crowd of the poorer class around it. These consisted mainly of British soldiers' wives and their dependants.'

There was no chance of getting in, and Robert and his brother Dan – and another Volunteer who chanced to come along just then – decided to walk to the distillery in Marrowbone Lane. The going was not easy. The rifle fire had got heavier and there were a few explosions, but at last Robert 'knocked at the big entrance gate to the distillery and a fellow from inside shouted out "Who's there?"'

Robert recognised the voice, and he was let in. Seamus Murphy, the Captain in the distillery, was in occupation of the building. He had about fifty men and fifty women with him there. This proportion of women to men was unusual for the Volunteers, but Seamus Murphy explained that, as neither Con Colbert, Éamonn Ceannt nor Dan McCarthy would take any of the women with them, they all had to come with him. Holland would have known most of them. They had all been to the Sunday night *ceilidhe* which Holland had attended the night before. When Seamus Murphy expressed his worries about his lack of men and rifles, Holland was very conscious of a 'big lot of stuff' and some fourteen men holed up in 'Mocky' Keogh's yard, which he had passed on his way to the distillery. Holland recalls that he was asked by Murphy: 'Was there any chance of [me] getting back there and bringing all the men and the stuff back with me. I said I would do it.'

It was decided that Holland would go to Mocky's yard with all possible speed and get back to the distillery with the men and arms:

I was then let out over the wall and I proceeded along the 'Back of the Pipes', which was a detour. I got back to Mocky Keogh's yard and reported to Joe McGrath (of

126

Hospitals Trust, still alive) and Philip Cosgrave (brother of Willie Cosgrave) and told them my mission. They immediately proceeded to get a horse and cart yoked up and they filled all the stuff into the cart. When I got back three other men had joined those already there. . . . When the horse and cart had been loaded up we pulled it out and proceeded down Cork Street at top speed, running. It was only a distance of about a quarter of a mile. We ran all the way, turned into Marrowbone Lane, and the gate of the distillery was thrown open and we entered, being received with cheers from the crowd inside.

The story of the battle of Marrowbone Lane Distillery was about to begin. Holland seemed to be reliving the events as he related them thirty-three years later:

It was about 3 PM when we arrived in the Distillery. They were all in good spirits there and they had posted the small garrison that they had to the best advantage, one man to each room. The rooms were like dormitories about 80 feet long by about 40 feet wide. These rooms were used as stores for kiln-drying wheat. The building lay between Marrowbone Lane at one end, Forbes Lane at one side and the canal in front. At the right-hand side was the 'Back of the Pipes'. There were eight windows on each side of each room with ceilings about 9 feet high. There [were] a lot of air ventilators in each wall about 12 inches from the floor level and these had small wooden shutters which could be pulled to one side. The walls of the building were about two feet thick, and we used the ventilators as portholes to fire out through.

When we arrived, Lieutenant Murray took command of us. There seemed to be more women than men in the garrison. In fact all the girls who were there were members of the Cleaver Branch of the Gaelic League and had been at a *ceilidhe* the night before. All these were also members of Cumann na mBan . . . Miss Cumiskey, who was, I think, in

127

charge, together with the wife of Captain Seamus Murphy, who was in charge of the whole garrison.

When giving his testimony, Holland scrupulously lists everybody's name, whether men or women. (It was certainly not his fault that the women were subsequently written out of the histories of the Rising.):

Josie and Emily O'Keefe, Josie McGowan, two Flaherty girls, two O'Byrnes, the three Cooney sisters (still alive) . . . the two Monaghan sisters.

All the men and women were put to work in a large circular room. Their first task was to fill a huge distiller's vat:

This vat had just been cleaned out and when we got there they were filling this vat with water, using hosepipes and buckets from all available taps. Both men and women were working at top speed.

But fourteen men, including Holland, were soon picked for other duties. They were well versed in the ways of Lee Enfield, Martini and Mauser rifles, and all were excellent shots. Holland was posted to the top floor, where he remained night and day for most of the week. He was given some brush handles and half a dozen hats and caps and put all these items at the windows for the purpose of deceiving the British soldiers and so drawing their fire. He described the position in some detail:

As one entered this room from a blank wall there were windows on my left which commanded a laneway called 'the Back of the Pipes', and Fairbrothers Field, which was about twelve acres square. This field bordered Guinness's buildings, Rialto, as far as Dolphin's Barn. In front and to my left was Cork Street. I had grand observation of both north and south sides of the canal banks, along the back of the South Dublin Union as far as Dolphin's Barn Bridge over the canal for about a half-mile. There were four windows and four ventilators to the front and I had a full view of Basin

128

Lane Convent, [the] Christian Brothers schools, Basin Lane and Basin Street, and of course the canal was in front as well. I could see all over the roofs of the houses in that area and in the distance . . . the South Dublin Union.

From his vantage point on the top floor, Holland could see a group of soldiers apparently trying to decide whether to scale or to breach the wall at the back of the South Dublin Union. He continues:

I loaded a Lee Enfield rifle and brushed away some grain that was on the floor, to lie down. I broke one of the ventilators. It was very warm and dusty in the room. I fired several rounds at the bunch of soldiers through the ventilator and kept firing at them as long as any of them remained there. This kept up for about an hour, and from what I could see a number of them were knocked out as they were lying on the canal bank.

Holland was aware that others were firing from the rooms above and below him, but it wasn't enough: he needed help. Josie O'Keefe, one of the Cumann na mBan members, was sent up to him with a can of water, a can of tea and some bread. She had been given charge of Robert and was expected to see that he had food and drink. He had an idea:

I told her to go down and if there were any spare rifles to bring them along and I would teach her to load them and leave them on the floor at my hand, as I might have to fire from either side of the building. She brushed away all the grain into the middle of the floor. I opened up all the ventilators and she went away and brought back with her a Lee Enfield and a Mauser and a haversack of ammunition. . . . I showed how to load the two rifles and she remarked how heavy the Mauser or Howth rifle was. She learned the job of loading them very quickly.

At about 5 PM, Robert noticed that the soldiers were preparing to attack 'in extended formation'. There followed an intensive

129

exchange of fire, which lasted until it was dark. By that time, another Cumann na mBan member, Josie McGowan, joined them, bringing another rifle with her. Thirty-three years later, Holland had little good to say about the Howth rifle:

> When the girls had gone I took off my shirt and left it off and put back on my coat and waistcoat. [The] 'Howth' . . . was a bad weapon for street fighting.
>
> Flame about three feet long came out through the top of the barrel when it was fired and a shower of soot and smoke came back in one's face. After three shots were fired from it, it would have to be thrown away to let it get cool and the concussion of it was so severe that it drove me back along the floor several feet.

The British began to take the Volunteers seriously: Holland reports that the former began to realise that 'it is a real fight and [they] are not leaving themselves so exposed to our fire.' The young defenders believed that all they had to do was to keep up the fight until the men from the country arrived. Optimistic rumours were rife in every Volunteer outpost. As Holland recalls, the distillery was no exception:

> I hear that all the country is marching on Dublin and it is only a matter of days until the job is done.

Robert's brother Walter, who was just fifteen – and who was, like his brother, a trained member of the Fianna – arrived with news of his family and more wildly optimistic rumours. In his statement, Robert relates what Walter told the assembled Volunteers:

> My father had collected some shotguns and ammunition in Joe Bowman's house in South Square in Inchicore and . . . my brother Frank was fighting in the South Dublin Union. He had heard that the Germans had landed in Galway.

When Walter had delivered his messages, he took off his celluloid collar (a removable collar commonly worn by boys during this period) so that Captain Murphy 'could write a dispatch on the inside of it to be delivered to Commandant Ceannt in the South Dublin Union,' Robert tells us.

Later, Walter returned with a cake for Robert, which his mother had made for his birthday. A messenger boy who was also a member of the Fianna dropped in six chickens. He worked in a poultry shop; the chickens, before they had been 'diverted', were meant for the officers in Richmond Barracks. The chickens – and the rumours – kept up the Volunteers' morale. The Company had inflicted fairly heavy losses on their attackers, and the British troops nearest to them had withdrawn for a time. Holland recalls:

> One of [the British soldiers] in particular ran all the way up to us and got as far as Forbes Lane when he was killed. We took in his rifle and ammunition. We then saw some stray army horses roaming about; one of them had the body of a Lancer soldier dragging along the ground and the dead man's foot was caught in the stirrup.

That night, when it had become really dark, Holland set off to forage for rifles:

> At 10 o'clock that night I crossed the wall and landed in a cottage garden next to the Distillery yard, where I picked up Walter and Mick Butler as arranged, at the entrance to the Back of the Pipes Canal. We crawled into Fairbrothers Field and made very slow progress and the time seemed very long before we picked out the first dead soldier. I cut off his web equipment and one of the others took his rifle. In this manner we stripped quite a lot of dead soldiers.

Holland and his comrades acquired more ammunition and at least ten rifles on this foray. When he returned to the distillery, he was sent to the fourth floor, where his fellow Volunteer Jack Saul was holding the position. Saul had heard a noise which he could not explain. Holland listened and:

> heard this noise like chains rattling. Something very heavy was being moved about. Saul shouted out 'Halt' but the movement still went on. I shouted 'Halt or I fire' and we

both shouted that we had it covered. We then decided to fire at the gate. Both of us fired and then a lot of confusion and noise ensued. A few minutes later Sergeant Kerrigan came up and shouted that someone in our wing had shot and killed 'Mocky' Keogh's horse. The horse had been rambling around the yard, nibbling the grass and throwing the collar and hames up around its head.

Whether Holland or Saul ever confessed to this unfortunate event we do not know. At any rate, Holland does not tell us.

Already things were beginning to wind down. Con Colbert, who was next in command to Éamonn Ceannt of this Company, had to evacuate the post he had held and withdraw to the distillery. Colbert was both very tired and disappointed with the turnout.

Their spirits lifted somewhat later on. Holland remembers:

On Wednesday about 10 AM a young man drove three two-year-old cattle down Marrowbone Lane. The gate was opened by Ned Neill and the cattle walked in. . . . I was told to kill one of the cattle, as I was then an apprentice butcher.

When he had butchered the animal, Holland 'dressed' it – and the garrison had meat as well as chicken for some days. He was then sent back to his post; it was only when the firing from the British side intensified and one of his friends was hit that Robert realised that he might be killed. By then, his brother Dan and 'big Jim O'Callaghan, Dan and Paddy Troy, Mick White, Mick Riordan, Arthur, Billy and Liam Power, Tom and Martin Kavanagh, Bob Young, Bill Kelly, Jack Saul and myself all had the two top storeys to ourselves.' As ever, Holland was meticulous in listing all of his comrades.

Like Domhnall Ó Buachalla and Seamus Robinson, Holland remembered the 'woman' who later turned out not to be a woman at all. When he shot her:

She sagged halfway out the window. The hat and small little shawl fell off her and I saw what I took to be a woman was a man in his shirtsleeves.

The battle wore on, and when darkness fell Holland and his friends were still manning the post. The firing eased off, and they then began to see the glow from the city. They got word that the city was on fire but were told that the British were suffering heavy losses, whereas the Volunteers had few casualities. This accorded with the experience of the garrison in Marrowbone Lane; extraordinary as it might seem to us today, Robert had no difficulty believing it. They were all in high spirits:

I and the rest of us had made our Easter duty and God would see us on the winning side. I was thinking all about my school days, the lectures that the Christian Brothers gave us each Friday from 12 o'clock to 1 about the Mass Rock and the Famine, of Blessed Oliver Plunkett and of Emmet and Tone, [Henry Joy] McCracken and the [Brothers] Sheares. All these came back to my mind in the dark of the night.

At dawn on Thursday morning, the British took up positions all round them. As Holland described it, they:

settled down to a 'battle royal'. All rifles are brought into play and Jack Saul, my brother Dan, Mick White and myself took up positions facing four different directions.

The young men and the women, who by this time must have become adept at loading the rifles, fought all that day. Con Colbert handed out hand grenades to Holland and the other marksmen as required, and that concluded the engagement for Thursday. Holland continues:

When I got on top again, the soldiers had become scarce but I could see a lot of bodies all around outside the wall and as far as Dolphin's Barn Bridge. I could just see a pit and Red Cross men working at it putting bodies into it at the bridge.

Friday morning came, and the weather was still fine and sunny. There was little firing from the British side. The Volunteers had time to talk. Holland remembers: 'There and then [they] made out

133

a list and checked up all the men of the Company.' It was easy to check under 'F', as the entries for this Company consisted mainly of a few families of brothers, the majority of whom were between eighteen and twenty years of age. Colbert was then about twenty-three.

Firing started again on Friday afternoon, and some troops spread into the fields round about. There was some exchange of fire but it died down again as darkness fell. (At nighttime there was generally little fighting, but there was some sniping, and a careful watch was kept.) Holland again foraged for rifles from dead soldiers. He later came down to the ground floor, where 'the usual rosary had started. When this had finished we had a talk with some of the girls, as we all knew one another.'

The women began to talk about arranging a *ceilidhe* for the Sunday night if they could get some kind of music. Holland remembers: 'Alice Corcoran said she would try and get her brother's violin if any of the Fianna boys would go for it.' But there was to be no *ceilidhe*.

On Saturday, the British troops withdrew out of rifle range. Otherwise, the day was uneventful. On Sunday, Robert was able to get an idea of the number of men and women in the garrison. He thought that there were about a hundred men and forty women. Around 6 PM, after the women had baked some cakes and were getting ready for the *ceilidhe,* a despatch came from Commandant Éamonn Ceannt at the South Dublin Union. A cease-fire had been ordered, preparatory to unconditional surrender. Half an hour later, Ceannt, a British army officer and a priest arrived. The ritual of surrender commenced. Holland recalls:

> Colbert blew his whistle to assemble his Company in the yard when all came down. . . . He brought us to attention and numbered us off. Ceannt, the British army officer and the priest had withdrawn to the front gate. Colbert then announced that we were surrendering unconditionally and that anyone wishing to go or escape could do so.

It would appear, according to Holland's account, that Colbert took a somewhat relaxed attitude to the protocols of surrender:

according to the rules of war, those surrendering should not attempt to escape. Be that as it may, Holland:

> had the distinct recollection of Joe McGrath (of Hospital's Trust) saying: 'Toor-a-loo, boys, I'm off.' He crossed the wall. Some others broke also.

Colbert re-formed the Company, with the Cumann na mBan women from the distillery at the rear. Holland reports that they marched down Marrowbone Lane and on to Cork Street, through Cork Street on to the Coombe, and up Patrick Street, turning on to Bride Road. On either side of Bride Street, the British soldiers stood two deep, with fixed bayonets. Machine-guns were posted facing them, and more British soldiers closed in behind them. At Iveagh Baths, Colbert surrendered his command, and a British officer gave the order 'for us to lay down all our arms on the road in front of us.'

This was a bitter moment for Holland, but worse was to come. When all the arms had been gathered up and thrown into a lorry, the Volunteers were marched back into Patrick Street. They turned on to Nicholas Street, then Christ Church Place, High Street, Thomas Street, James Street, Mount Brown and on to Kilmainham. Holland remembers:

> At this point a crowd had gathered. It would then be about 8 PM and was falling dusk. At Kilmainham we were jeered at and as we passed by Murray's Lane both men, women and children used filthy expressions at us. 'F' Company, which was mainly made up [of men from] Inchicore, heard all their names called out at intervals by the bystanders. They were [shouting] 'Shoot the Sinn Féin ——s.' [*sic*] My name was called out by some boys and girls I had gone to school with, and Peadar Doyle was subjected to some very rude remarks. The British troops saved us from manhandling. This was the first time I ever appreciated the British troops, as they undoubtedly saved us from being manhandled that evening, and I was very glad as I walked in at the gate of Richmond Barracks.

The fight was over, and Holland was sick at heart. On Tuesday, the Company were again marched down the quays to the North Wall, from where they were shipped to England in the hold of a cattle boat. On disembarking, they were sent by train to Knutsford Prison in Cheshire. In August, Holland was transferred to Frongoch in Wales.

Thirty years later, what rankled most with Holland was the help that had been given to the British army by the men who worked in the Great Southern Railway Works at Inchicore. In his statement, he relates that he presented a photograph of an armoured car, built by these workers, to the 1916 Museum at O'Connell Schools. He identifies the men in the photograph and – as ever with Holland – gives their names. Then he gives us a different list: the names of their workmates who fought as members of the Volunteers:

> Joe Bowman, Peter Doyle, Ned O'Neill, Joe Downey, Bill and Dan Troy, Arthur, Bill and Liam Power, Tom and Martin Kavanagh, Tom Young, Bill Kelly, Joe Gorman, Mick White, Paddy Byrne, Fred Foye and Mick Fox.

Few of the witness statements are as detailed as Robert Holland's, and fewer still resonate with as much hurt: he felt rejected by people he had known since childhood. Although Frank Robbins describes similar events, he talks of the pride he and his companions took in the fight, which had ended in unconditional surrender rather than the reactions to the putting down of the Rising from many Dubliners:

> We had failed in our object; others had failed before, and they had not been ashamed or afraid of the consequences. Why should we?

If they truly felt like that, Robbins asserts, they could face the hostility:

> of the vast majority of the citizens. . . . Little did we think that the Dublin citizens would ever go so far as to cheer British regiments because they had as prisoners their own fellow citizens – Irishmen and Irishwomen – just as they were.

11

'We Got It Hot'

Joseph Furlong was a Wexford man and a member of the IRB. At the time of the Rising, he was acting as an undercover man for the IRB. He took his instructions from Michael Collins. Furlong and three others had been brought over from London because of their special skills as toolmakers. Their instructions were to return to Dublin and find employment in firms which were important to the British war effort. They had no difficulty in doing this: they all got jobs at the shell factory in Kingsbridge (near what is now Heuston Station), which was run by the British armed forces.

As IRB men, Furlong and his comrades automatically joined the Volunteers, but they did little or no training. Instead, they continued to work at the factory right up to the week before the Rising. Furlong tells us that, on Easter Monday, at about 1 PM:

> A runner came and told us we were to report to Jacob's factory, getting there any way we could. He also told [us] that the GPO was already taken.

The men were a little late getting to Jacob's. On the way, they met a priest who took off his hat and blessed them, but they also met 'with a lot of opposition from the wives and daughters of British soldiers, who were known as the "Ladies of the Separation Allowance".' (This referred to the payments made by the British government to the wives of soldiers in the British army.) Jacob's had already been taken by the Volunteers when Furlong and the others finally arrived, and they had to get in through the window. Thomas MacDonagh and John MacBride were there. Ignatius

Callender, who had been advised by Father Augustine OFM Cap. to write up his account of his part in the Rising while it was fresh in his memory, had received special instructions from Sean McDermott for John MacBride. There was no danger that MacBride, a Boer War veteran, would miss the Rising.

MacDonagh presented Furlong with his own 'Peter the Painter' (an obsolete gun); the gun was brand new, Furlong remembers. In his witness statement, he describes some of the fighting at the factory. He threw a grenade, with little effect. There was some sniping from the British side, as well as machine-gun fire, but compared to the engagement at Marrowbone Lane, little happened:

> Food was plentiful, including some meat and tea. We supplied the Garrison of the College of Surgeons and the Turkish Baths with food from Jacob's.

From where they were positioned, the men in Jacob's could hear the firing of the artillery in the centre of the city. They could 'see the glow of fires in the skies', Furlong recalls.

On Sunday morning, they saw Thomas MacDonagh and John MacBride leave the building:

> After a long spell we were told to parade down in one of the lower rooms and there MacDonagh and McBride told us that we were to surrender and the fight was over. They told us that Pearse had surrendered and that the GPO and Liberty Hall were destroyed and all O'Connell Street was in ruins.

Despite some initial reluctance to obey this order, when MacBride spoke to the assembled men, pointing out the necessity of what he and MacDonagh had asked them to do, they all agreed to follow the orders. They were marched out to surrender, under the command of Jimmie Shields:

> who was one of the youngest of the garrison. . . . [The British] lined us up on the street with our weapons on the ground.

The following Wednesday, they were marched to the cattle boats at the North Wall to be shipped to England.

Con O'Donovan fought at the Four Courts during Easter Week. On Holy Saturday, he was one of the men detailed to guard Bulmer Hobson in Martin Conlon's house. O'Donovan knew well the real purpose of the manoeuvres that had been ordered for Easter Day. After the plans were hastily changed following MacNeill's countermand, O'Donovan was chosen to dispatch the new orders for the Rising, which was now to take place on Monday. O'Donovan had some difficulty mobilising his full complement of Volunteers, as most of them had gone to the Fairyhouse Races. He was sent to guard the side gate to Chancery Street near the Four Courts. By Tuesday, O'Donovan was, he recalls:

> in some informal fashion accepted as leader. One poor fellow, who was certainly very unfitted for soldiering, even of the mild kind we were experiencing up to Thursday, became so unbalanced from the strain that I had to get him down to the ground floor, with a request that he be kept there, and given a rifle again.

On Thursday, the Volunteers were shelled:

> Then came a shattering explosion, and the room trembled. Their first shell hit rather low between the two windows of the room I was in. We had not enough sense, or military training, to retreat.

Eventually, they:

> made their way to the ground floor, where we found our comrades praying for us as dead.

The order to surrender reached O'Donovan and his comrades on Saturday.

Maurice Collins was one of the other men chosen to guard Bulmer Hobson. He was not able to join the Rising until word came to his party that they were to release their prisoner. Collins made haste to take up his post 'in Lamb's public house, first floor, at the corner of North King Street.' This was an outpost of the Four Courts where Ned Daly, Tom Clarke's brother-in-law, was in charge. They came under heavy fire almost immediately and had to withdraw to the Four Courts on Friday evening.

'On Saturday, notice of surrender reached us,' Collins recalls. He describes the events of those days briefly and dispassionately:

> Later that night [Saturday] the Four Courts garrison were marched in a body to the Rotunda Gardens. We stayed for the night in the open and we marched the following morning to Richmond Barracks, where the prisoners from all the other garrisons throughout the city were assembled. . . . Here I remained for a fortnight, and during this time many of my comrades were being picked out for court-martial or deportation by members of the G Division. . . .
>
> On the morning that we had received orders from the British that we were to be deported, I was standing beside Sean McDermott in the Barrack Square and said to him, 'It looks, Sean, as if we will be all together wherever we are going next time.' He replied, 'No Maurice, the next place you and I will meet will be in heaven.'

That evening Collins was shipped to England, to be imprisoned in Wandsworth Jail. He never saw McDermott again.

Collins had a stroke of luck when he was released from prison in December 1916. Before the Rising, he had been a civil servant but his dismissal notice did not reach him until December. He remembers:

> It so happened that I received pay from Easter Saturday up to Christmas Week 1916 through an oversight on the part of some official, as he failed to inform me at the proper time of my dismissal. I then went into business as a

tobacconist and confectioner with a billiard room attached at 65 Parnell Street.

From 1916, these premises were used extensively by Michael Collins. Maurice Collins and Michael Collins were close friends, the former recalls:

This friendship started when we were both in London and continued to the end until Collins's death on 22 August 1922.

James Foran took a remarkably independent view of his role in the Rising and what was expected of him. Having located Éamonn Ceannt, he stuck with him on his way to the South Dublin Union:

I went home and got ready and I let on I had to go on a parade. I took my brother-in law's bicycle, he was after paying ten shillings for it. All the kids were there and asked me, 'Where are you going?' 'I am going off to the war,' I said. I went over to the Square and there was a crowd in the Square, and I put the bicycle against the wall and went up to Ceannt, who said, 'You had better come with me', and I said, 'Yes I will.'

Ceannt led his group to the back entrance of the South Dublin Union, where they forced an entry. Foran was given charge of the front gate of the Union. He was not to let anyone in except Tommy McCarthy, who was to deliver ammunition.

'Right,' said James. But there was no attack from the British and things were 'a bit slow' for Foran. He remembers:

At about two o'clock or so on Monday, Cathal Brugha came down and said that the soldiers were getting in over the wall and he wanted a couple of men. I said, 'I'll go, because there is nothing doing here. I will get a shot up there.' I was going when some of the fellows upstairs shouted down that Ceannt sent me there and that I was not to be taken away. Two other men went up, and they were not very long up there when the two of them were shot dead.

But Foran fought on for the rest of the week, creating barricades using books and ledgers – which were readily available in the South Dublin Union. On Thursday, he decided to move from the front gate back to Headquarters, located in the Nurses Home. They had to go through a couple of buildings to get there.

Foran, as ever ready to tell a story against himself, describes what follows:

> We started to burrow from room to room. Eventually we came into a room, in which there was a whole row of doors and presses all along, and we tried two or three of them but they were all presses. I said, 'You had better start over here.' We started to break a hole at the corner and we were halfway through when some fellow went over and turned a handle and there was a door there all the time, after us breaking through the wall.

The fighting at the Volunteer Headquarters came to an end on Saturday, and the surrender took place on Sunday. Foran and William Cosgrave went out to meet Thomas MacDonagh, accompanied by Father Aloysius and Father Albert, who had come with the terms of surrender:

> We fell in that Sunday evening in the Union Yard. The English Major was walking up and down, and said, 'Mr Ceannt, when will all your men be out?' Ceannt answered and said to him, 'These are all the men I have.' There were only thirty-two men, to the best of my knowledge.

All in all, Foran was very glad he had 'turned out' for the Rising, despite the fact that he was subsequently sent to prison. He had thought of making a break for home on the march to Marrowbone Lane but:

> It was a good job I did not go home because there were thirty soldiers occupying the house.

He was sent to Knutsford Prison, where, he tells us, 'nothing happened'. The part that he played in the Rising, and in the 'troubles' which followed, proved to be very bad for his paint business. This business did not really recover until his boys – the same boys who had asked him where he was going, on the Easter Monday when he left for the 'war' – 'started to get going', as he put it.

Thomas Slater, who had been a member of the IRB since 1905, fought the Rising under Thomas MacDonagh, who was in charge of the 2nd Battalion. The general plan was, as Slater noted in his statement, 'for the main body to take over Jacob's factory with outposts' (buildings that served as bases from which the Volunteers fanned out to other positions).

On Easter Monday morning, Slater's superior officer in the Volunteers, Tom Hunter, called to Slater's house. Slater recalls:

> He had written instructions from Tom MacDonagh to mobilise the Battalion at Father Matthew Park and that the men of the Battalion were to get to Stephen's Green before 12 o'clock. They were not to march there as a unit but to proceed there individually and in groups. . . . I then went round and mobilised in Fumbally Lane and Camden Street, presumably to link up with the Citizen Army, who appeared to be trying to get to Portobello Barracks or to prevent anything from coming down [from the barracks].

An earlier plan to take Trinity College was called off by Thomas MacDonagh, and the plan to take the Telephone Exchange in Crown Alley was not carried out. All in all, Slater appears to have seen more action than Joseph Furlong. By the time he made his statement, Slater was unclear about the exact order of events, but things were clearly not too comfortable where he was during the latter part of the week. He remembers:

> On Thursday or Friday, I am not sure which, we sent out a patrol of about twelve men under the command of Lieutenant Danny O'Riordan to try and make contact with

143

other units or find exactly the disposition of the enemy. On returning, fire was opened on them from Harcourt Street and I think from Grafton Street, and a Volunteer named O'Grady was shot. They carried him into Jacob's, and on examination it was found that he was seriously wounded. He was brought over to the Adelaide Hospital and was taken in, but he died the following day. He was a young married man.

When the patrol arrived back they reported that they had failed to make contact with any other unit of Volunteers, and that they 'were more or less compelled to come back as they were being fired on.'

Some Citizen Army men arrived at Jacob's on either Wednesday or Thursday. They did not stay, as they were anxious to join their comrades in the College of Surgeons, which the Citizen Army men were still holding. Slater was glad to record that the garrison at Jacob's was able to send provisions to the garrison at the College of Surgeons. The order to surrender came on Sunday. Slater is brief on this point:

On Sunday morning Father Augustine and Father Aloysius came to Jacob's to inform us that Pearse had surrendered. MacDonagh decided to go with the two priests to ascertain the truth for himself. He would not surrender until he got definite orders. Meanwhile he told every man that could, to get away, as there was no use of lives being lost. Everybody that could, got out. There was a great deal of confusion and a lot of recrimination that we were surrendering without having been in action at all. MacDonagh left, and a good lot of us cleared out and got away. That was the last time I saw MacDonagh. I managed to get home and was never arrested.

As we have seen, if we are to believe the evidence given in the witness statements, observance of the protocols of surrender was somewhat variable amongst the leaders. For instance, Con Colbert permitted flight as he announced the imminence of unconditional surrender, and Joe McGrath fled. Bob Price, who made no effort to do so himself, encouraged 'very young lads and the older married men with dependent children who were not in uniform to try to get away.'

In contrast, Patrick Ward, a member of B Company, 3rd Battalion, under the command of Commandant Éamon de Valera, was left in no doubt whatever about the correct procedure when one's Company was about to surrender.

Ward was one of those who almost missed the Rising. He had got married in February 1916 and moved to Sandymount, and he had subsequently contracted pneumonia; as a result, he had lost touch with his Company. He received no mobilisation order either on Sunday or Monday and had no idea that the Rising was about to happen. In his statement, he remembers:

> The first intimation I had that something unusual was hap-
> pening was the general rumour which I heard on my way to
> lunch on Easter Monday. That evening my wife and I decid-
> ed that we should get back if possible to my wife's home in
> Sandwith Street and that she should stay there until further
> notice.

He quickly established contact with people who were in close touch with the Volunteers and was advised to wait until Tuesday morning if he wished to take his place with his Company in Bolands Mills. On Tuesday morning, he met a Volunteer called FitzGerald. Ward recalls:

> He brought me through the Distillery, up a ladderway from
> the top of the Distillery building on to the platform of
> Westland Row Station, where I proceeded along with
> FitzGerald to report to Sean MacMahon in Bolands Bakery.

He fought at various posts throughout the week:

> The last day and night – that was Saturday and Sunday – I
> spent on sentry duty with Joe McDermott in a room over

Commandant de Valera's headquarters at the back gate of Bolands Bakery facing out to the top of Clarence Street.

On Sunday, it was all over, although the Volunteers were not aware of it. Ward remembered the morning clearly:

Sunday morning was exceptionally quiet. The weather was sunny and fine and there were all sorts of rumours of forces marching to relieve the city and even that there was a possibility of a German landing. This made the announcement [of the surrender] around 12 o'clock all the more staggering. All the outposts were called in to parade in the flour stores of the bakery. We were paraded [and] brought to attention and Commandant de Valera announced that we were to surrender. He made it plain that this was an order he had received himself and which he was passing on as an order. It was possible in the position we had held, not being by any means surrounded on all sides, for the whole garrison to leave by the railway and proceed home quietly, but this would not fulfil the terms of the surrender, and Commandant de Valera stated, as we had gone into battle on an order, the order to surrender was equally binding.

De Valera saw it as essential for the soldiers under him to surrender under orders in order to enhance the status of the Irish army and the Republic.

It was Saturday afternoon before the Citizen Army garrison at the College of Surgeons heard anything about surrender. Some of the officers began to discuss what they might do in the event of a surrender being ordered. Frank Robbins tells us that:

the question had been discussed and projected plans arranged to fight our way past the British cordon on the bridges out to the Dublin hills, where the fight would be carried on along the lines of guerrilla warfare.

At first, Robbins could not believe it when the suggestion was made that all men with uniforms were, if possible, to obtain civilian clothes so that they could perhaps escape. When word came that the Volunteers fighting in the GPO had surrendered, the dispatch was read out:

> Commandant Mallin in the course of his address said it was quite possible for a number of the men and women then present to get back to their own home, should they desire to avail of the opportunity, and nothing the worse would be thought of them for doing so. . . . A small number of those present took the opportunity of getting away.

According to Sean McGarry, who was very close to Tom Clarke, the possibility of escape was at least considered by the Volunteers fighting at the GPO:

> While negotiations were going on, Tom [Clarke], seconded by [Sean] McDermott, suggested that some of us could escape. I decided to stay but I passed on to several [of my comrades] that there was a way out. I remember telling Luke Kennedy, who availed himself of what he regarded as permission, and escaped. I do not know how many, or if any, others did the same.

The protocol for surrender was a matter of some concern to the survivors of 1916. Whether they followed it or not, the scrupulous observance by the Volunteers as a whole of the terms of surrender demanded by de Valera became a matter of pride, as did the time the Volunteers spent in jail. There was, however, reason in all things, and if a particular individual became separated from the rest of his Company, as Desmond FitzGerald did when he escorted the wounded from the GPO when the fighting was coming to an end, it was quite in order that that individual not go through the ritual of surrender with one's defeated comrades. FitzGerald did not give a witness statement but in his *Memoirs,* first published in 1968, he tells a gripping story of his escape. FitzGerald does not appear to have taken any serious steps to evade capture and was easily picked up by the RIC when he returned to his home and family in Bray.

147

An equally enthralling story is told by Tom Byrne, a veteran of the Boer War, who had delivered the Kildare men led by Domhnall Ó Buachalla safely into the GPO so that they could take part in the Rising. Tom Byrne also escaped but was not captured.

Thomas Leahy had left Dublin well before the Rising. He was a shipyard worker, and there was not much demand for his particular skills in Dublin. He secured employment as a riveter in Barrow-in-Furness in England, working on submarines. He was a member of both the Volunteers and Sinn Féin and kept in close touch with his comrades in both organisations in Dublin. Irish nationalists kept a low profile in Barrow-in-Furness, and when war was declared in 1914, they had to be particularly careful. Much of the work that he was engaged in was war-sensitive. In his witness statement, he explains:

> It was decided that those who [could] get home before restrictions on leaving the port came into force should do so, and keep in touch with those with houses and families for years in the town, who would help in every way by securing arms and explosives and collecting money for purchasing of same.

Leahy travelled to Dublin in November 1914 and immediately secured work at the Dublin Dockyard. He joined the Irish Volunteers, E Company, 2nd Battalion, based in Phibsboro in Dublin, where he met Oscar Traynor, Sean Russel, Tom Weafer and Harry Boland, amongst others. Traynor was his Section leader; Leahy had huge respect for him. Leahy was immensely proud of his battalion and of its commanding officer, Thomas MacDonagh.

Leahy describes in some detail the unease caused by Eoin MacNeill's countermanding of the Sunday manoeuvres, but this setback was forgotten when certain of their number were given their orders after being mobilised at Liberty Hall. They were ordered to attack the magazine fort in the Phoenix Park. Leahy remembers:

The guard were to be disarmed, their arms taken, and [they were to be] tied up in the guardroom. Personnel were to be attacked, the keys of arms and ammunition stores taken; some of the arms and ammunition were to be destroyed, and as many of the arms as could be taken by us were to be collected by [a] motorcar, which would be in attendance for same. After playing about with a football for some time, to put the sentry then passing the top of the wall off his guard, we sat down in a group and each man got his instructions, and if successful, to report at the GPO, O'Connell Street, which at that time we did not know was to be our headquarters. We moved off in order, after saying a decade of the Rosary.

They did succeed in reaching the GPO – albeit with considerable difficulty, as one might imagine. Leahy found people on Lucan Road discussing the noise of the arms exploding; all along the way, British troops were active. He joined his battalion at Annesley Bridge in Fairview; the battalion retreated to the GPO, taking supplies of food with them. They were made welcome at the GPO but, Leahy remembers:

After a brief address we were then given orders to take over all shops and premises to the corner of Abbey Street from the Hotel Metropole.

Leahy and his fellow Volunteers proceeded to break their way through the buildings, erecting barricades and posting men at the windows and 'all advantage positions for defence'. Meanwhile, 'the mobs from the back streets were busy smashing windows in the big shops and looting everything they could get their hands on.'

Leahy was one of the very few witnesses who made any excuse for the behaviour of the Dublin populace:

Their long suffering under the economic conditions and low wages for their labour made them determined to grab all they could. It was a pity to see them.

149

The men from Ballybough experienced some stiff fighting. They were lucky to have with them a Boer War veteran called Vincent Poole, whose experience – and sense of caution – were a great help to them. Periods of quiet alternated with 'terrific' firing. Leahy recalls:

> We found out that the British troops had crept into the [Dublin Bus Company] building . . . from the corner of Eden Quay and had also taken Hopkins and Hopkins jewellers' shop. We got it hot from then onwards and our men from that side of the street began to make dashes over to our side, for the buildings started to take fire and very soon the whole place was a huge inferno with maddened horses rushing about that had escaped from burning stables. . . . Suddenly we got word from Oscar Traynor that we had to retire to the GPO for instructions.

But the GPO was itself on fire, and the Volunteers who were already there were about to evacuate.

12

INSIDE THE GPO

When the Rising began on the amended date – Easter Monday instead of Easter Sunday – the Volunteers had no Chief of Staff, according to Jack Plunkett's witness statement. Jack Plunkett was a brother of Joe Plunkett, who was a signatory of the 1916 Proclamation and was executed after the Rising. According to Jack Plunkett:

> Joe's position at the time of the Rising was Director of Military Operations. He was not appointed Chief of Staff in place of Eoin MacNeill, nor can I say that MacNeill was ever formally deprived of that position at any meeting of the Military Council before the Rising. If I heard that he was, I have forgotten it now.

Sean FitzGibbon, who was a close friend of Eoin MacNeill, according to his witness statement, held that:

> The Rising was not planned, organised, or even discussed by the Executive of the Volunteers.

At any rate, the Rising began without the Chief of Staff. The Proclamation was read and the GPO was occupied. But well before publication in the Sunday Independent of MacNeill's counter-manding order, John Twamley had made his preparations for his own special role in the impending struggle. In 1916, Twamley was a linesman in the Engineering Department of the Post Office and was stationed in Bray. At a special meeting of the IRB Centres held in North Frederick Street earlier in April, he and several other selected men were told of the coming Rising. They were, according to Twamley:

> asked to get all possible information regarding the location of cross-Channel trunks [main phone lines] and to obtain plans of all underground cables and secret wires running to Dublin Castle and [the] Viceregal Lodge. We were told to try to obtain the tools necessary to lift manhole covers and to cut stays, poles and wires. The information obtained was to be submitted to Dermot Lynch. We were allotted areas in which to work. I was given Bray.

Twamley was a useful man to have in such an enterprise. He knew all about trunk lines and where they could be severed. A Mr Higgins of Bray was also a member of the IRB. Through him, the Volunteers were able to see a plan, in the county-council offices near Shankill, of the Bray area; together, they marked the relevant points and discussed how best they could cut the communications of the British forces. Everything was ready when they were called together at Liberty Hall and told that the Rising would take place on Easter Sunday. They had even been able to get keys for the manhole covers.

When Twamley got the news at about 11.40 on Sunday morning that the Rising was off, he went at once to Liberty Hall, where Dermot Lynch told him to hold on for further orders. Twamley recalls:

> On Easter Monday morning between 9 and 10 o'clock I got an order to report immediately to Liberty Hall. . . . The Rising was taking place at 12 o'clock and . . . I was to go to Bray at once.

When he reached Bray, Twamley could not contact any of his men, and he lost a good deal of time frantically trying to find them. At last, he met Higgins and was able to tell him to mobilise his men and get them to the GPO at once. There was no time to spare. He himself ran across the fields to the railway, 'climbed the poles and cut the telegraph and telephone wires and all the railway signal wires.'

Then he went on to the road and cut the wires between Shankill and Bray, as well as the underground cable at Shankill. On his way back to Dublin, he called in to the Lamb Doyle's for a drink. Nothing untoward happened until he arrived at Rathmines Road near the Barracks. The military were on duty there, so he changed course and went in to the city through Rathgar; he reached the GPO without difficulty. Dermot Lynch – who had already heard that Twamley had cut the lines in Bray and was well satisfied with his contribution – met him there. He was immediately given the job of seeing that the men got food and rest in preparation for the military action to come.

Some hours before Twamley arrived on Easter Monday 1916, the Rising had formally begun. Just before noon, the members of the Provisional Government travelled in an open touring car from Liberty Hall to the GPO. The car was driven by The O'Rahilly, and Patrick Pearse and James Connolly sat in front. The GPO was seized without a shot being fired. The touring car was used during the week to get supplies from Findlaters.

The men who fought in the GPO and gave their witness statements to the Bureau of Military History years later had a very clear recollection of what they witnessed during the week, but they would have had difficulty in stating what happened on a particular day – as Leahy's and Harris's accounts make clear.

Many of the witnesses had been posted outside the building from time to time, and others were instantly deployed elsewhere. Charles Saurin, who had managed, with great difficulty, to get into the GPO, was sent back again to Fairview. He recalls:

> I heard later that Pearse was exceedingly perturbed at our arrival from Fairview when he was apparently under the impression, which may of course have been given to him by [Tom] Weafer, that we were remaining on the outskirts of the city as a kind of holding force.

Later in the week, James Connolly sent for Saurin and his Company, who had earlier come to the GPO from Fairview. This came as a great relief to a bored Saurin, who had found little to do at Fairview.

Eamon Bulfin, an early member of the IRB and a Lieutenant in the Rathfarnham Company of the Volunteers, gives an extremely comprehensive account of his week in the GPO. Early on Monday morning, he received the order to get his Company together. They boarded a tram at Rathfarnham; the tram stopped at the corner of Dame Street and Georges Street and they marched the rest of the way to Liberty Hall. They found no one there but, just then, received an order to proceed to the GPO immediately. They procured a handcart for all their equipment and set off for the GPO. Just as they reached the entrance to Princes Street, the Lancers came down O'Connell Street. The Lancers were fired on from the GPO and from the Imperial Hotel across the street. In the confusion that followed, Bulfin was able to find:

> a small window about four feet from the ground, on the side of the Post Office. I broke the window with my rifle, and incidentally broke my rifle. Any chaps that were near me, I called them out by name and 'hooched' them up the window. Jack Kiely was actually on his hands and knees on the windowsill, when he was hit by a bullet. . . . We brought the wounded man into the Post Office. We got into the sorting room but there was no one there and the door leading into the main hall was locked.

Bulfin shot the lock off the door. He and his men reported to Commandant Pearse and were ordered to take up a position on the roof. Bulfin continues:

> We held that position all the time until Wednesday evening. A Franciscan or Dominican, or a priest of some Order, gave us conditional absolution on the roof on Monday morning. I did not see him again.

Although Louise Gavan Duffy – one of the first secretaries of the Cumann na mBan – had heard numerous rumours, she had no idea that there was going to be a rising. She recalls:

I was tired hearing rumours and . . . I went out to see what I could see.

She describes her journey from Haddington Road to the GPO. She was not hindered in any way and heard no shooting: it was too early for that. She arrived at the GPO and asked to see 'Mr Pearse'. She continues:

I was brought into the Post Office and I saw Mr Pearse. He was as calm and courteous as ever. I now think it was very insolent of me because I said to him that I wanted to be in the field but that I felt that the Rebellion was a frightful mistake, that it could not possibly succeed and it was, therefore, wrong. I forget whether he said anything to that or whether he simply let it go. He certainly did not start to justify himself. I told him that I would rather not do any active work; I suppose what I meant was that I would not like to be sent with dispatches or anything like that, because I felt that I would not be justified. He asked me would I like to go to the kitchen.

So Gavan Duffy spent the week of the Rising in the kitchen of the GPO. She worked extremely hard – so hard, indeed, that she was somewhat vague when describing what she did and saw there:

I suppose I began to wash up, or cut bread and butter then. I did not see very much. We came down once or twice during the week perhaps, but we were very busy and we did not get invitations. When we were not working, we were resting. We did go to sleep. . . . I remember going to sleep on a mattress in one of the corridors.

When Min Ryan gained entrance to the GPO, with the help of Sean T. O'Kelly, she did not get to see Sean McDermott, who was resting, and returned home to Ranelagh without having seen him. Later, she was glad of this, she says. (If she had not gone home, she would have missed meeting her brother Jim.) She and her sister Phyllis waited for Jim, who had not yet returned from Cork. He arrived in the afternoon. Min Ryan recalls:

The three of us walked down the whole way to the GPO along by Trinity College – Jim, Phyllis and myself. I remember, when I was passing by Trinity College, I had a feeling that there was something serious going on there. You would see an old man peeping out from behind sandbags or you would see the muzzle of a gun.

This time, she *did* see McDermott:

We saw Sean McDermott in a small room off the main office and he made us come in and sit down. I said, 'I suppose you will kill me for taking MacNeill's message.' He said, 'It won't make any difference. I know in my heart and soul that they had wanted to fight.' I think it was the mercy of God that it was like that. If we had [had] a big Rising, we would have had a lot of destruction.

Like Gavan Duffy, Ryan was sent to the kitchen and put to work carving large quantities of beef for the men:

I remember carving, carving. Very likely, girls came in and took the meat around to the men. The men did not come up to our room to eat, but remained at their different posts. Desmond FitzGerald was there. I knew him fairly well.

That same evening, Min Ryan recalls, 'Tom Clarke wanted to have a talk with me and with Miss [Kathleen] MacMahon.' The two women were presumably chosen by Clarke because, as women, they were unlikely to be shot by the British in the event of the Rising being put down and would therefore be able to explain the Rising and why it happened after he had died. Ryan recalls:

Tom Clarke told the same story to each of us. . . . The gist of it was – that people naturally would be against them for rising and coming out like this, that one of the reasons for people being against them would be because of the countermanding order, but that they had come to the conclusion that it was absolutely necessary that they should have this Rising now, because if they did not have it now, they might never have it; that when the men had been brought to a certain point, they had to go forward, that in any case a rebellion was necessary to make Ireland's position felt at the Peace Conference so that its relation to the British Empire would strike the world. I asked him, 'Why a republic?' He replied, 'You must have something striking in order to appeal to the imagination of the world.'

Clarke also held, according to Ryan's account, that the shedding of blood had always raised the spirit and morale of the people:

'Of course,' he added, 'we shall all be wiped out.' He said this almost with gaiety.

Clarke had achieved his lifetime ambition of fighting for Ireland. He was able to tease poor Sean McGarry, who adored him:

Tom Clarke said, jokingly, to him: 'Miss Ryan will get you a cup of Bovril. She gave one to me; it is great stuff.'

In his witness statement, Sean McGarry takes the opportunity to defend his hero from the disparaging remarks of Frank O'Connor. McGarry comments:

He [O'Connor] says in his book *The Big Fellow*: 'Old Clarke, harassed and excited, was blaming everyone for the mistakes which had been made.' Now I have no idea when O'Connor got that picture, for I can with certainty say that it is an utterly false one.

Louise Gavan Duffy continued her work in the kitchen. All the days ran into one for her:

I did know when Friday came, but the other days were all the same. There was nothing outstanding until the fire came in front and we saw the flames out of the window.

Tom Harris remembered something similar, when he and the

other Kildare men led by Tom Byrne returned from the Exchange Hotel to the GPO:

> We went back to the Post Office and it was like one long day – I have no recollection of sleeping. On the first night I was at one of the windows, for another period I was on the roof. I remember being in the Instrument Room, where it was first noticed that the Post Office was on fire. The ceilings were arched. You could hear the guns going and I saw a little hole, just a circle, which came in the plaster, about the circumference of a teacup, and I could see this growing. It was evidently caused by an incendiary bomb.

Min Ryan was not in the GPO when the fire broke out. As well as working in the kitchen, she was sent to deliver various messages. The wives of prisoners had to be told of the prisoners' whereabouts. But she remembered what the general scene in the GPO was like:

> The Headquarters people were not doing any fighting in the GPO. They were watching things. Pearse spent most of his time in the front part of the Post Office. It was nearly the same then as it is now, although it has since been done up new. There was more or less a front passage. There was a counter where you could get stamps. All these young fellows – the Plunketts, Mick Collins and crowds of others, including the members of the Larkfield Camp – were manning the windows. The Headquarters staff sat there talking quietly. The Howth guns made a lot of noise, but it seemed that these young Volunteers enjoyed firing away. Gearoid O'Sullivan, who was high in rank, was inside all the time. Pearse sat out there in the front on one of the high stools, and people would come and talk to him.

Jack Plunkett describes the huge effort put in by Connolly – almost as if Connolly wished to make up personally for the gaps in the chain of command in the GPO and the O'Connell Street area:

The Chief of Staff should be familiar with his subordinates, and Connolly was not. My opinion is strengthened by the fact that Connolly several times left the Post Office to go and see how the fighting was progressing elsewhere.

The Chief of Staff would be enjoined to get in touch with other areas, and we know that Connolly got out of the GPO a few times to explore the surrounding areas.

Seamus Robinson expresses a certain irritation with these interventions. On the Thursday morning after he had reported the sighting of the British boat engaged in shelling Liberty Hall, he received an order which, he was told, came from Connolly, to evacuate Hopkins and Hopkins. By the time this situation was straightened out, the position could only be retaken with great difficulty.

When Eamon Bulfin and the other Volunteers had been relieved of their duties on the roof on Wednesday, they were brought down to the ground floor and put to work strengthening the barricades at the front, from where an attack was expected to come. Bulfin recalls:

> For the barricades we used sacks of coal up from the cellars and a lot of great big books, as far as I remember.

Joseph Scollan missed the end of the fighting in the GPO. On Thursday morning, Connolly asked him to go to Broadstone Station to find out what was going on there. Scollan had barely arrived there when he was picked up by British soldiers, who kept him in custody until the end of the week.

Seamus Robinson found his way back to the GPO around midday on Friday. He remembers:

> The houses on the opposite side of O'Connell Street were all on fire and one building [had] completely caved in. It was at this time that I remember the first shells hitting the roof of the GPO. They were incendiary shells, and despite the efforts of some of the Garrison to control the fire with hosepipes, the fire spread and more shells were landing on the roof.

A decision to evacuate seemed inevitable, but before that certain preparations had to be made. Robinson recollected that:

> Volunteers were called for, to remove explosives from the main hall to a cellar or room downstairs. I was one of the volunteers engaged on this work.

Another who volunteered for this work was John Twamley. The Volunteers moved the explosives to a strong room in the basement and laid a fuse where the fire would catch and explode the material after the building had been evacuated.

Louise Gavan Duffy thought that she and her comrades were 'going to stay in the building until we died. . . . I did not ask [whether this was the case] and nobody told me.'

On Friday morning, Gavan Duffy heard that they were evacuating the building. Before she left, she spent some time taking down the names and addresses of men who were to remain in the GPO so that she could deliver messages to their families. Somebody decided that she and Desmond FitzGerald were to go to Jervis Street Hospital with the wounded. She did not know who had decided this, neither did she know who had told them to leave the GPO via the Henry Street exit. She relates:

> There were holes broken through the walls. There is a yard at the back of the GPO, I think, and some of the men must have gone out beforehand and prepared the way. They must have climbed up the wall at the back, on to some low roofs, then on to the gable end, and smashed a way in to the nearest house, and from that to the next house and from that to the next house. They went through about three houses, and these houses were in Henry Street. There was a tiny little theatre in Henry Street, with a stage. I think it was the Coliseum.

She thought Dr Jim Ryan was probably in their group but had no very clear recollection of whether he was or not. Somebody carried a Red Cross flag in front of the little procession as it made its way to Jervis Street, where the wounded were taken in to the hospital. The women were told that they could lie on the floor for the night. The British took the men who were not wounded away.

Next morning, Gavan Duffy heard about the surrender. She recalls that she was surprised:

> I did not know when we were leaving that they were going to surrender. I thought that they were evacuating the Post Office and going somewhere else. I certainly did not have the impression that it was all at an end.

She was right. When the Volunteers retreated from the GPO, the leaders of the Rising had not yet decided to surrender. Eamon Bulfin remembers the events of Friday night, when things were surely approaching the end:

> It was duskish . . . when we were all ordered in to the main hall. When we had assembled there, we were addressed by Pearse. I don't remember his exact words. We were ordered to take as much food and ammunition as possible with us, and to try and get in – as far as I remember now – to [the] Williams and Woods factory. I did not know where it was at the time.

Thomas Leahy remembers those last few hours in more detail:

> Orders were given to make for a lane opposite in Henry Street, in batches, at short intervals, for a heavy machine-gun post was very much in action from somewhere about Jervis Street. That was the first time that we . . . had heard of the wounding of Commandant Connolly, who had to be carried across the bullet-swept street together with the other wounded and all the arms and useful material to enable us to carry on. [The stretcher bearing Connolly] was successfully carried out just before the roof fell in in flames. On reaching the lane, we found ourselves outside a mineral-water factory, which we entered. And this gave a welcome respite to all, especially the wounded.

At this point, it was decided that the Volunteers would have to do something about the machine-gun post from which the British were firing on them. Jack Plunkett recalls:

> When The O'Rahilly met his death, he was leading an attack on the barricade on the top of Moore Street.

The Volunteers gained entry to the house on the corner of Moore Street and Henry Street, and there was a call for volunteers to bore through the walls of the houses as they had done in O'Connell Street earlier. Oscar Traynor addressed Leahy directly, the latter remembers:

> 'You are a boilermaker or shipyard riveter, and used to heavy hammers, and we must get through those houses, so you can get started. And myself, [Vincent] Poole, [and Harry] Boland will help all we can.'

They all worked very hard indeed – so hard, in fact, that Seamus Robinson almost fell asleep whilst still wielding his crowbar. Next morning – Saturday – Robinson recalls that:

> When I awoke it was completely dark and everything was quiet. I was utterly exhausted and, feeling around the darkened room, I came into contact with a vacant bed. I rolled into bed and again fell fast asleep.
>
> When I awoke the next time, it was daylight. There were sounds of firing some distance away. I got up and moved through the buildings towards an end house. There was [sic] a number of Volunteers there, including George Plunkett. We could see a British barricade nearby. A party was lined up to rush the barricade when orders came that we were not to fire on any British soldiers until further orders. I think it was Sean McDermott who brought this order to us.

The Rising was over.

*

162

Sometime earlier, Domhnall Ó Buachalla had become separated from the main body of his comrades fighting in Henry Street. He eventually ended up at Broadstone Station, where he was captured by British soldiers. For his part, Tom Harris was put out of action just as the Volunteers were preparing to evacuate the GPO:

[Ted] O'Kelly called on me to help him give out the rations and I had not a dozen rations given out when I got a bang on the foot. I was wounded and O'Kelly got a slight wound. I think some fellow let off a shot and I got the most of it, and that put me out of action. They all evacuated and I was carried out into Henry Street and down Moore Lane. Henry Street was then under fire, but they got me through. I was on a stretcher. Two fellows carried me and I was in a stable in Moore Lane for that night.

Tom Byrne had left the GPO on the Thursday, on James Connolly's orders. Byrne recalls:

I was ordered to take about ten men and occupy a corner house on Capel Street.

It was hopeless. Wherever the Volunteers turned, they were met by armoured cars or troops. On Friday morning, Tom Byrne decided that the game was up. Byrne continues:

There were a couple of young men with me who were deserters from the Dublin Fusiliers, and they asked me, seeing that the fight was over, would I give them a chance to make their getaway, as it would be very serious for them if they were caught fighting with us. This was on Friday. I saw the force of their necessity and let them go.

That evening (Friday) I said to the others, 'It's all over now, there's no use trying to retreat to the Post Office. Each of us can now make his getaway.' I forget where we dumped our arms.

Byrne was not taken prisoner. Instead, he crossed the street:

with Jack Kenny and a couple of others, and we went into an old furniture premises. No one would ever suspect us [of] being in this house. I went upstairs. There was no one in the house. I went in there and got something to eat, and also a moleskin trousers and an old jerry hat. I changed my clothes and, with a few days' growth of beard on me, looked quite the part of an ordinary 'navvy' or working man. That night I could see British officers outside the door and hear them talking.

And so Tom Byrne went 'on the run'.

On Friday, Min Ryan made one last effort to get back into the GPO:

It was very difficult. I tried, in a most stupid way, to get back. I went to a main street and along by the College of Surgeons. I could have got into the College of Surgeons, but it never occurred to me to do so, as my mind was bent on getting to the Post Office. I turned back then, when I found it impossible – when I saw a dead dog at my feet. The College of Surgeons was all pockmarked from a machine-gun placed on [the roof of] the Shelbourne Hotel. It was in front of the College of Surgeons that I saw the dog being shot. It ran out in front of me and suddenly it lay on the ground. It could have been myself if I had walked on another bit. I went home then.

*

Shortly after 10.30 on Friday morning, a fierce battle began at Ashbourne in County Meath. At that time, the RIC barracks was situated about half a mile north of the village. John Austen, to whom we are indebted for his eyewitness account of this little-known engagement, was well-placed as a witness. He worked for the Post Office, delivering telegrams and messages. He was aware that the police had phoned RIC Headquarters earlier that morning and that the garrison near Ashbourne had been reinforced. He positioned himself with a few others on Lime-kiln Hill, from where he had a good view of the fighting when it began. Austen and his companions saw Thomas Ashe and some of his men 'arriving there on bicycles, with guns on their shoulders.' Austen reports:

> Tom Ashe came walking down the road and went to the Barracks and asked the police to surrender. . . . The police refused to surrender. Ashe went back to his men, got them under cover, and the battle began in earnest.

The Volunteers fought from behind walls and fences, taking advantage of every physical feature of the landscape:

> Some of the rebels got on to the footpath along the road, behind the fence in front of the barracks, and behind the fence on the opposite side of the road, whilst some others were on the north side of the Barracks. Some were behind a wall which was on the south-west side of the crossroads.

The fighting was fierce. Ashe lost two men: one was killed outright, and the other died later of his wounds.

But it was the RIC who suffered the heavier casualties. When the battle was over, Austen went back to the road. Someone asked him to take the dead men away. He got a horse and cart and proceeded up the road. He remembers:

> I told Ashe what I was going to do, and he told me to go ahead. Two of the policemen who had not been wounded helped me to collect the dead policemen into the cart. I had eight dead men in the cart when I had finished. Included in this number were Sergeant Shanagar from Navan and Sergeant Young. Two of the dead men were civilians who I believe were drivers of cars. . . . The police had twenty-seven casualties all told.

Next day, the coffins arrived for the dead policemen; after the bodies had been placed inside, the coffins were taken away in a lorry. By that time, Ashe and his men had returned to their camp at Borranstown, County Meath, taking their 'two men that were killed and wounded away with them,' Austen reports.

13

The End: Executions

After Louise Gavan Duffy had had a wash, a good sleep and a meal on Sunday morning, she felt fully refreshed and was keen for news of how the Rising was going. She went to Min Ryan's home in Ranelagh, where about seven or eight people were already gathered. Gavan Duffy gave them the news that The O'Rahilly had died and the others had surrendered. Ryan and Gavan Duffy decided that they would go to Jacob's to see Thomas MacDonagh, who was commanding the garrison there. He was out when they came. When he returned, Gavan Duffy felt compelled to tell him what she thought about the Rising, just as she had earlier felt compelled to tell Pearse:

> I said to him that it was all over, that it should not have taken place, that it was wrong and could not have succeeded. He said to me, 'Don't talk to my men if that is the way you are feeling. I don't want anything to be putting their spirits down.'

As the two women left Jacob's, they saw the surrender at the College of Surgeons. According to Gavan Duffy, there might not have been more than twenty Volunteers there; they looked utterly dejected. Ryan remembered talking to the prisoners; the two women were able to take messages from them to their families.

Dr Kathleen Lynn and Helena Molony, both members of the Citizen Army, had seen little action, but on Tuesday they were taken prisoner in City Hall. Helena Molony writes:

> Towards evening, we saw a large Company [of British soldiers] – probably a hundred men – going into the Castle. I believe they got troops in rapidly through Ship Street too. There was now a large garrison in the Castle. At about half past eight or nine o'clock, when nightfall came, there was a sudden bombardment. It came suddenly on us – on the roof level on which were glass windows, and through the windows on the ground floor of the City Hall, there were machine-gun bullets pouring in. From the ceiling the plaster began to fall. It was dangerous.

It certainly was dangerous. When the soldiers began to break the windows at the back and to come through them, the men and women of the Citizen Army knew the game was up. The women, who were on the ground floor, were taken out one by one through the window by British soldiers. Other women were upstairs. Molony delights in telling us that:

> The British officers thought the rebels had taken these girls prisoner. They asked them, 'Did they do anything to you?' 'Were they kind to you?' 'How many are up there?' Jinny Shanahan – quick enough – answered: 'No, they did not do anything to us. There are hundreds upstairs – big guns and everything.'

Naturally the officers were very angry when they found out that they had been fooled.

The prisoners were brought to Ship Street, where the women were put in a large room, which, it seemed to Molony, was underground. Dr Lynn remembered seeing 'the people passing above through a grating.'

The food was bad and the sanitary arrangements were appalling. They slept on thin little mattresses called 'biscuits'; worst of all, these mattresses were infested with lice. Molony would never forget them:

There were old bits of mattress on it, used by the soldiers. They were covered with vermin; and before a day had passed we were all covered with vermin too. I did not get rid of them until I went to Lewes Jail; and even the baths in Lewes Jail did no good. Dr Lynn used to put us through a de-lousing drill every day.

There were advantages to being imprisoned in Ship Street, however. The room in which the women were held was right on the street. Molony was able to get a girl to change a five-pound note for her. Moreover, Ship Street was close to where some of the girls' families lived. The soldiers too were quite friendly. Molony recalls that:

The Dublin Fusiliers were there. They would bring us in a dish of fried bacon and bread.

Even before the executions took place, the British soldiers' attitude towards the rebels was not universally hostile. Tom Harris, who was wounded in the GPO, describes how he fared at the Castle Hospital:

In the surrender we were carried out and a number of other wounded too. We were placed at the side of Moore Street. The garrison . . . marched out of Moore Street. I think Mick Collins was in charge of them. . . . The street was deserted for a short while and then we noticed military appearing and we were carried down to the end of the street and into Parnell Street. The ambulances were waiting there and we were taken to the Castle Hospital by Dr Houghton. He is attached to the Orthopaedic Hospital. All the principal surgeons of Dublin came in that time – Sir William Taylor, Stokes, etc. We were well treated there and we were all in one ward. Cathal Brugha was also there.

Eilis Bean Ui Chonaill, a member of Cumann na mBan, had worked in the more traditionally female role as nurse and general support to the fighting men of the Rising. She was first deployed in Reiss's Chambers on O'Connell Street and later in Church Street, at the first-aid station in Father Matthew Hall. The Volunteers provided plenty of food for the Volunteers in the hall; it was there that Eilis tasted tomatoes for the first time in her life. As well as tending the wounded, the women carried food to the men on the barricades in Church Street. One of the Capuchin Fathers accompanied them on their rounds. Ned Daly, whose sister, Kathleen, was married to Tom Clarke, commanded the battalion in this area. Eilis Ui Chonaill describes the end of the Rising:

> As the week came to a close, the fighting became more intensive and it became very difficult to get out to collect the wounded. Some were carried in to our hall by their comrades and some – the more seriously wounded – were carried to the Richmond Hospital close by.

When night fell, the Cumann na mBan moved all the wounded into Richmond Barracks, on stretchers. Eilis Bean Ui Chonaill continues:

> Sir Thomas Myles was in charge. When we had brought in the last of the stretcher patients, he put his hand on my shoulder and I thought he was going to have me arrested. But he just asked whether we had got any sleep during the week. I said no and he patted me on the shoulder, saying we girls had done Trojan work with the wounded.

Mairín Cregan noticed a slight flicker of awakening sympathy from the people assembled in a waiting room in Mallow railway station. She shared the waiting room with several other passengers who were waiting for a train which would take them at least part of the way to Dublin. (Due to the Rising, the trains were not running to normal timetables.) When she gave her statement, Cregan had no idea on what day she had left Kerry for Dublin, but it was probably Wednesday of Easter Week. She had been told that Dublin-bound trains were getting only as far as Ballybrophy in County Laois. She recalls:

> Rumours were rife and I remember one cold and miserable evening, while in the waiting room of the station, a man

came in with yet another [message] that 'The military [have] mown down the Volunteers in front of the GPO.' I, being worn out with fatigue and frustration, began to cry. To give an idea of the attitude of the general public at that time, who apparently did not realise the significance of the Rising in Dublin, one of those present turned to console me, saying, 'It is only the Sinn Féiners that were killed.' This enraged me and I turned on them, saying, 'But it is the Volunteers I am crying for. My friends are among them and fighting too.' It was remarkable that in a very short time, first one and then another began to murmur, and the little crowd began to argue and take sides.

This was the first public expression of sympathy for the Volunteers that Cregan had experienced.

Back in Dublin, the Citizen Army women continued to endure their prison conditions. Dr Lynn remembered with horror:

We had dusty grey blankets which were all crawling with lice. I never slept during the time I was there. I could not. The scratching . . .

Like the great majority of the men who had fought on the nationalist side in the Rising, the women were moved from Ship Street to Richmond Barracks. From there, they were taken to Kilmainham Jail. Dr Lynn was able to get rid of the lice at last.
And then came the executions.

William T. Cosgrave, later President of the Executive Council of Saorstat Éireann, gives an excellent account of the processing of prisoners in Richmond Barracks, including some of those who were to be tried by court-martial. Cosgrave had held the post of Lieutenant in the 4th Battalion in 1916 and had fought in the South Dublin Union under the command of Éamonn Ceannt. After the surrender, as a prisoner, Cosgrave was in close contact with the many Volunteers whose witness statements are quoted in this book. His description of the routine which the defeated insurgents imposed on themselves in prison is an intriguing glimpse of a culture which still survived in the Ireland of 1949 when he made his statement:

> While in Richmond Barracks prisoners' quarters, we were locked up at 8 PM. Shortly after that the Rosary was recited and everyone settled down for the night. This did not require any special arrangement, as there were no beds or bedclothes, rugs, blankets or other impedimenta. John MacBride told me on one of those nights that his life-long prayer had been answered. He said three Hail Marys every day that he should not die until he had fought the British in Ireland.

William Cosgrave, John MacBride and Éamonn Ceannt were selected for court-martial on the same day, 4 May 1916. When William Cosgrave, his brother Phil Cosgrave, MacBride and Peadar Doyle heard that they were to be escorted to Kilmainham Jail, they asked that Father Augustine OFM be sent for when the time came. Ceannt was left behind, as his trial had not yet finished. The prisoners arrived at 8 PM. Each prisoner was allotted a separate cell. William Cosgrave recalls:

> Phil Cosgrave got the cell on my left, the Major [John MacBride] on my right. At daybreak on Friday morning I heard a slight movement and whisperings in the Major's cell. I heard the word 'Sergeant', a few more whispers, a move towards the door of the cell, then steps down the corridor, down the central stairs. Through a chink in the door I could barely discern the receding figures; silence for a time; then the sharp crack of rifle fire and silence again.

Dr Lynn found the time she spent in Kilmainham Jail harrowing:

Madame Markievicz was overhead in the condemned cell and we used to hear reports that she was to be executed. We also heard about the other people that were being executed. We could hear the shootings in the mornings, and we would be told afterwards who it was.

After about a week in Kilmainham, Dr Lynn and her comrades were moved to Mountjoy Jail. In Mountjoy, she found herself more involved in the heartbreak which followed the executions. She recalls:

We discovered that when the suffragettes were there, they had made little holes in the plaster under the pipes so that, if one lay down on the floor, one could talk to the person in the next cell. Countess Plunkett was in the next cell to mine. Of course, she was in a terrible state about her son having been executed, and she used to get awfully lonely and upset at night. We would lie down on the floor and talk, and that would make her better.

Joe Plunkett, a signatory of the 1916 Proclamation, was executed soon after the Rising. His sister Geraldine Plunkett married Tom Dillon just before the Rising. It had been originally planned that Joe Plunkett and Grace Gifford would get married on the same day, but the former decided to postpone his marriage. These were busy times for the Plunketts. Joe Plunkett had been sent to America in September 1915 by the IRB. When he returned, according to his sister Geraldine:

The gland in the centre of his right cheek began to get troublesome. He had to stay in bed a good deal.

At the same time, their mother, the Countess, was in America lecturing. Shortly afterwards, their sister Mimi was sent to New York with dispatches. On a second visit, she was delayed in New York and stayed there for the duration of the Rising. Their father, Count Plunkett, went to Rome in April. He was entrusted with the task of counteracting the representations made by the British Envoy to the Vatican. The Count had some success in this. When he returned to Ireland, he visited several bishops; none of the bishops he interviewed subsequently condemned the Rising. Joe, Geraldine and Mimi's brothers George and Jack were in charge of the Volunteer Camp at Larkfield in Dublin.

When her fiancé, Tom Dillon, got his mobilisation orders on Holy Saturday, Geraldine Plunkett was dumbfounded. She had not expected anything like this to happen until May. The couple married (in the sacristy, because marriages were not allowed in church during Lent) and took up temporary residence in the Imperial Hotel opposite the GPO. She remembers:

> From the window of the front sitting room we occupied in the hotel, we had a complete view of everything.

Geraldine Plunkett tells us that they saw the Company of Volunteers led by Pearse, Connolly and McDermott marching into the GPO, the Volunteers bringing in food and erecting barricades, and the attack of the Lancers and their retreat, leaving the dead horse on the street behind them. The Plunketts left for Larkfield on the Tuesday. By the end of the week, their friend Rory O'Connor had begun to think it likely that not only Joe Plunkett, but also George and Jack, would be shot. Count Plunkett was arrested on the Monday 1 May. She tells us:

> My mother filled her handbag with Woodbines, and with this passport got through cordon after cordon and got to the vicinity of the Castle with a view to making a row and getting the boys off. But she failed to reach it. She was arrested next day.

News of the early executions began to filter through to family and friends. Patrick Pearse, Thomas MacDonagh and Thomas Clarke were shot on 3 May.

Reverend Father Aloysius, a Capuchin priest from Church Street, made a detailed account, based on notes he made at the time, of his own pastoral and spiritual involvement with the leaders of the Rising in the days leading up to it.

The Capuchins in Church Street were called in by the military chaplain in the first week of May. It seems that James Connolly, who was imprisoned in the Castle hospital, had expressed a wish to see Father Aloysius. The Father went to the Castle, where he saw James Connolly and heard his Confession. On that first occasion, he was invited by the officer in charge, Captain Stanley, to attend to the other Volunteer leaders, as Father Aloysius describes in his witness statement.

> Late on Tuesday 2 May I had just gone to bed – fairly exhausted and expecting a good rest – when I was called to learn that a military car was at the gate and a letter was handed to me, telling me that Prisoner Pearse desired to see me and I had permission to see him, and that, failing me, he could see any other Capuchin Father. With that I accompanied the military and we drove in the direction of Charlemont Bridge. The sniping from the roofs was so fierce that the car did not venture to proceed further, and turning back, we went direct to Kilmainham.

When they arrived at Kilmainham, Father Aloysius learned that Thomas McDonagh also had need of his ministrations:

> I heard the Confessions of Pearse and MacDonagh and gave them both Holy Communion. They received the Blessed Sacrament with intense devotion and spent the time at their disposal in prayer. They were happy – no trace of fear or anxiety.

Father Eugene Nevin, a member of the Passionist Fathers, based at Mount Argus, in Harolds Cross, Dublin, describes how Mrs Pearse, the mother of Patrick and Willie Pearse, came to Mount Argus every day from the start of the insurrection. It fell to Father Nevin to break the news of the deaths of her two sons to her.

The night before Thomas MacDonagh was shot, a message was brought to his wife, Muriel, by a private soldier. Muriel was a sister of Grace Gifford, who was to marry Joseph Plunkett. Thomas

MacDonagh was shot on Wednesday morning, and Joe Plunkett was to be shot on Thursday.

Grace Plunkett gives us her own account of those few days:

> I went out one day, and the papers had the news that MacDonagh and Pearse, and somebody else, had been executed. The next morning, although we had been up all night, I woke up as if I were being pulled out of bed by an unseen force, and dead beat after being awakened. I dressed and went to the priest; and I told him Joe was going to be executed. . . . I went down to a man, named Stoker, to get the wedding ring. He lived opposite the Gaiety. I went to Kilmainham, then to see Joe. . . . I was let in to see him; and the prison chaplain must have been there; and he married us.

Next day, Joe Plunkett was executed. Years later, Grace Gifford's heartbreak was still as real as it had been on that May morning in Kilmainham:

> He was not frightened – not at all, not the slightest. I am sure he must have been worn out after the week's experiences, but he did not show any signs of it – not in the least. . . . I was never left alone with him even after the marriage ceremony. I was brought in, and was put in front of the altar; and he was brought down the steps; and the cuffs were taken off him; and the chaplain went on with the ceremony; then the cuffs were put on him again. I was not alone with him – not for a minute.

That night Grace saw Joe again to say goodbye. She was allowed to stay for only a short time. She clearly regarded this as unfair:

> I believe that Min Ryan and Father Browne were allowed to stay a long time with Sean McDermott. Min Ryan was there with Sean McDermott for ages and ages.

Possibly the most poignant story of pain and grief from this time is that told by Geraldine Dillon, Joe Plunkett's sister and Grace's sister-in-law. The subject of the story is Count Plunkett, Grace's father-in-law. Geraldine Dillon recalls:

> During my first visit to Richmond Barracks, my father told me that the day Joe was court-martialled, he saw him standing in the rain below in the barrack square. He knew he was to be shot, and they gazed at each other for about half an hour before Joe was moved off. My father was weeping as he told me this.

Sean McDermott was one of the last of the Rising leaders to be executed. On 11 May 1916, an army driver handed Min Ryan a note. She remembers that the note said that:

> The prisoner, Sean McDermott, would like to see me and my sister, if she would like to accompany me. We had to call to the North Circular Road to collect Sean Reynolds and Sean MacDermott's landlady.

The party of four had about three hours with McDermott – excruciating hours for Min Ryan. The presence of Sean Reynolds and the landlady precluded privacy, Ryan remembers:

> We were all there together, listening to each other's conversation. He was very anxious to have the others go. He was much more intimate with us, but there was no budge out of them. 'That is all now,' Sean would say, but there was no budge at all. Then we all came out together.

It must have been difficult for Min Ryan to claim any special consideration for her evidence, or even to offer it. She was not one to talk of her special relationship with Sean McDermott, except in the most indirect way. Monsignor Patrick Browne, who knew both Sean McDermott and Min Ryan well, gives his opinion in his own witness statement:

Anybody meeting him [McDermott] that time would not say he was a man doomed to die soon. He spoke about Min Ryan. She was his sentimental attachment – seriously. I think that was serious.

Min Ryan's spare and economical account nonetheless clearly expresses her great pain. There is little doubt about her relationship with Sean McDermott, and she, more than most, knew of his leading part in the Rising. Ryan had tried to get back into the GPO on Friday, but this was impossible. On Saturday came news of the surrender and the burning of the GPO. Ryan continues:

I could not tell you really very much after that. Sean McDermott was not shot until the 12th [of May]. We thought he was going to escape. I wrote an article in a paper in America, which I will hand in. It gives exactly my impressions at the time I went to see Sean McDermott. This was the morning he was executed. We were there at 12 o'clock and remained till three. He was shot at a quarter to four.

Min Ryan's son Professor Risteárd Mulcahy, in his biography of his father, *Richard Mulcahy: A Family Memoir,* reproduces part of the article to which Min Ryan is referring:

At four o'clock on that Friday morning a gentle rain began to fall. I remember feeling that at last there was some harmony in nature. These were assuredly the tears of my Dark Rosaleen over one of her most beloved sons.

Aine Ceannt, who was so deeply in her husband's confidence right up to the beginning of the Rising, had said her goodbyes to him on the Easter Monday morning, just before he set out to take command of the 4th Battalion. She describes their last few minutes together:

Turning to [their son] Ronan, who was watching us, he kissed him and said, *'Beannacht leat a Ronain',* and the child replied, *'Beannacht leat a Dhaide.'* *'Nach dtiubhraidh tu aire mhaith dod mhaithrin?'* he asked. *'Tiubhrad, a Dhaide,'* said Ronan, and so they parted forever. ['Goodbye Ronan.' 'Goodbye Dad.' 'And won't you take care of your mother?' 'I will, Daddy.']

I would have wished to go to Emerald Square to see the men march off, but Eamon asked me not to, and so I embraced him, bade him God speed, and he went out.

During the few days leading up to Éamonn Ceannt's execution, the information given out by the authorities was cruelly misleading. The night before the execution, Aine had about twenty minutes with him, in the company of his brothers and sister. She recalls:

As I was still in doubt as to the outcome of the morning, I remained up all night with my sister-in-law, and each hour we knelt down and said the Rosary. From three o'clock I remained praying until about half past five. . . . We made our way down Church Street. It was a glorious summer morning, and when we arrived at the Priory I asked for Father Augustine. He sent down another friar, who told me that Father Augustine had only come, celebrated Mass and gone to his room, but that if I wished he would get up and come down to me. I said no, that I only wanted to know the truth, and this priest said, 'He is gone to heaven.'

Nora Connolly O'Brien had missed the Rising. Just before it started, she had been sent north by her father with messages for Denis McCullough and Dr Patrick McCartan. Connolly O'Brien and her Cumann na mBan comrades left on the ten o'clock train. But the leaders did not respond to the messages. When Connolly O'Brien and the other messengers arrived on Easter Monday, the assembled Volunteers had been dispersed at Coalisland and other centres, where they were meant to be ready to take orders. It was Thursday before she managed to meet Dr McCartan. They had a bitter discussion, at the end of which Connolly O'Brien was in no doubt:

It was quite definite that nothing was going to happen – that they were not going to fight in the North at all.

So the women decided to return to Dublin. They got as far as Dundalk by train and travelled the rest of the journey on foot. When Nora pointed out to the others that they could not travel by night, she remembered her sister saying:

'Pick out a nice warm field, and stay there until it is light.' And that is what we had to do; and certainly it was not warm. I think that it is the first time I realised all the bones there are in the body.

When at last they reached Dublin and heard from Padraig Ryan's sister that the fighting was over, it was an awful shock. The last of the 1916 insurgents had surrendered a few hours before. James Connolly had been wounded and was in prison. The sisters immediately thought of their mother Lily, who was out in Madame Markievicz's house at Three Rock at the foot of the Dublin Mountains. They walked through the ruined city on their journey to find their mother:

I remember seeing all the ruins. There was one big ruin, in the shape of a cross, just swaying as if ready to come down. In Cathedral Lane, there were dead horses, and everywhere a terrible smell of burning buildings and some rubber.

When they got to the cottage, their mother had made her mind up. She was quite certain:

'I know they won't let him live. As long as he is alive, there is a chance of it [another rising] starting again.'

The whole family – Lily and the five girls – was taken in by William O'Brien. Their brother Roddy, aged fourteen, had been arrested and was still in custody. Connolly O'Brien remembers:

We learned that Daddy was in the Castle. Mama went to the Castle to see him.

Nora saw him on the day he was court-martialled. She knew her mother was right. If they were prepared to court-martial him while he was in bed, they would be prepared to execute him.

A few nights later, the summons came, and Nora and Lily were brought in an ambulance to see him for the last time. Nora recalls:

Mama could hardly talk. I remember he said, 'Don't cry, Lily. You will unman me.' Mama said, 'But your beautiful life, James.' She wept. 'Hasn't it been a full life? Isn't this a good end?' he said. Then they took us away; and we got home. We just stood at the window, pulled up the blind, and watched for the dawn; and after we knew he was gone, the family all came in; and I opened the last statement, and read it.

Nora stood there in the cold light of the dawn and read her father's final statement out loud:

We went out to break the connection between this country and the British Empire, and to establish an Irish Republic. We believed that the call we then issued to the people of Ireland was a nobler call, in a holier cause, than any call issued to them during this war, having any connection with the war. We succeeded in proving that Irishmen are ready to die endeavouring to win for Ireland those national rights which the British Government has been asking them to die to win for Belgium. As long as that remains the case, the cause of Irish Freedom is safe.

Believing that the British Government has no right in Ireland, never had any right in Ireland, and never can have any right in Ireland, the presence in any one generation of Irishmen, of even a respectable minority, ready to die to affirm that truth, makes the Government forever a usurpation and a crime against human progress. I personally thank God that I have lived to see the day when thousands of Irish men and boys and hundreds of Irish women and girls were ready to affirm that truth and to attest it with their lives, if need be.

14

THE AFTERMATH: INTERNMENT

The executions, which continued over two weeks at daily, or slightly longer, intervals, made an enormous impact on the people of Ireland. The country was in a state of shock, and in the space of just a few weeks sympathy for the rebels began to increase. It is against this background that thousands of nationalists were transported to British prisons. These included people like Eoin MacNeill, who had done more than most to prevent a Rising taking place at all.

Comparatively few of the witness statements dwell on the witnesses' experiences in prison. It was as though the fighting, the surrender, and the fate of their leaders had drained them of all emotion. Most simply list the prisons where they spent some time. The statement given by Seamus Robinson is an example:

> On Sunday we were marched to Richmond Barracks and were lodged in a large gymnasium. We were passed individually through an interrogation room, and a number of us were lodged in parties in large barrack rooms, the rest deported that night. In my room were Padraig Ó Maille, Joseph Gleeson, Joseph Derrham, Seamus Mallin, M. W. O'Reilly, Barney Mellows, Frank Fahy, Major MacBride and, I think, A. P. Reynolds. I remained in Richmond Barracks for about a week and was then deported to Stafford Jail, Frongoch, and on to Reading.

Thomas Leahy describes the change for the better brought about by the intervention of the famous Dubliner Alfie Byrne, who was then MP for North Dublin. The War Office had decided to give the Irish prisoners the same treatment as that afforded prisoners of war. There were great changes in prison life as a result. Thomas Leahy's description of life in Knutsford Jail reads like something from the better kind of schoolgirl's story from the early part of the twentieth century:

> After a day or so, visitors began to be allowed in, and many were girls from a convent school near to hand, and they never spared themselves for us, above all in getting into touch with our families in Ireland and letting them know all our wants etc. At the time there was a very large number of the boys who were taken prisoner who had their uniforms on them – as all they stood up in. They were wanting to get them home as they were told they would have to hand them over and that other clothes would be provided. No one liked that, as the uniforms had been bought out of their own pocket money and, besides, they had a sentimental value to all of us, and we were determined that they would not be given up, even if we had to go naked. This was explained to the girls on the next visiting day and their help sought; so it was arranged between us that two or three would be taken out at each visit and they would come in with a suit or trousers and jacket under their own clothes, and a group would be formed while one girl was removing her clothing etc and the uniform donned in its place. Likewise the same change with the owners of the uniforms going out, which were all delivered safely to the homes for which they were intended, thanks to the services of these great-hearted girls.

What amused Leahy and his comrades was that it was evident that the prison authorities knew that something was going on, but they could not fathom what. After each visit by the girls, the prisoners were counted and recounted. They could get the right number of men – but not of uniforms.

When the last of the wounded had been deported from Dublin, the British authorities decided to move the bulk of the Irish prisoners to Frongoch, an internment camp in north Wales. The convent girls were broken-hearted. Leahy was one of the advance party sent on ahead to get the place ready. The camp was an old distillery, which had already been pressed into use as accommodation of German prisoners.

Leahy and his friends lost no time in setting up structures which would ensure the smooth running of the camp – almost as though it fell to them to demonstrate to the world, and to themselves, that they were indeed soldiers. They took their orders from their own officers, whom they elected to the camp council. Working parties, selected each day, carried out the various duties essential for the health and welfare of the prisoners. In spite of the fact that the large rooms were infested with rats, one suspects that Leahy enjoyed his time in Frongoch. Prison life there was not simply a matter of keeping oneself and the accommodation clean. He recalls:

> Classes were formed on every subject in everyday life that would be expected of us under the law under the Republic. We hoped to confirm at the first chance after release all departments of government business, and instructions to fit men capable to take over these departments when required.

The prison camp included a piece of ground, which the prisoners used for all kinds of sport. Football, running and jumping kept the men fit. In time, the guards became friendly with the prisoners, and the former were always pleased to attend the concerts which the prisoners held in the dining hall on Sunday nights. Looking back on his days in Frongoch, Leahy had no doubt of the importance of this time in the history of the next few years. He continues:

> Had the British government known what was taking place under their own guard and officials, we would have been hunted out of the camp, for it must be realised that men came together in that camp from all parts of Ireland; from towns, villages and places that would have taken years to

bring together for the work which had to be done, especially in the training of the army of the Republic.

It would seem that there was just enough friction between the prisoners and the authorities to make life interesting for Leahy and his friends. For example, the authorities sought the names of those amongst the prisoners who were liable for military service because of their birth in England or Scotland. No one betrayed these individuals, and the camp council, Leahy recalls, fought the military:

> the whole road, and many concessions were stopped to force our hand. Men like Dick Mulcahy (now General) took up this case and not one of them was ever found.

Towards the end of the year, the men began to be released in dribs and drabs until there were only a few hundred left; these men were to be kept in the camp until Christmas:

> It made a great difference in the rooms, for they were lofty and cold. Myself, Dick Mulcahy and Arthur Shields (now a film star) had to close our beds together to try to keep warm, and many were the interesting chats on the future struggle took place after lights out. Little did I dream then I would be fighting against him in the Civil War when it came.

The men set about making Christmas truly memorable. They wrote to their families asking them to send any extra luxuries they could afford; they cleaned the whole camp and put up decorations; they cooked the good things that were sent from home.

Suddenly, they were informed of their imminent release, on 23 December – giving them no time to enjoy the celebration they had prepared. What would they do with the good food? But the camp authorities and the camp council came to a satisfactory arrangement: the British army bought most of the food.

Thomas Leahy made it home for Christmas.

For someone who had missed the Rising, Ernest Blythe built up an impressive prison record. Shortly before Easter 1916, certain of the most prominent Volunteers, including Liam Mellows and Ernest Blythe, were deported to England. The Volunteers made every effort to get them back. They were successful with Mellows but not with Blythe. Helena Molony remembers:

> About February 1916 I was sent over to England. That was the only mission I was sent on, either abroad or at home. I was sent by Sean McDermott to arrange the return of Ernest Blythe, who was in open arrest in Abingdon, England. I did not see him on the morning I arrived there. When Blythe went to report to the police that morning, he was kept by them.

Blythe was sent to Oxford Prison, where Mabel Fitzgerald, Desmond FitzGerald's wife, visited him with orders that he was to put up a defence and make every effort to secure his release. The services of George Gavan Duffy, a half-brother of Louise's who practised as a solicitor in England, were engaged for that purpose. Blythe was indeed subsequently released but arrested again and kept in Abingdon Barracks for ten or so days – during which time the Rising took place.

Blythe was moved from Abingdon Police Station to Brixton Prison. There he saw Roger Casement in the prison church on the second Sunday of his stay in the prison. A few days later, he met Casement again, this time as he was coming round a corner in the company of some warders. On this occasion, Blythe was able to shake him by the hand.

It was two months later before Kate FitzGerald, a sister of Desmond's, was allowed to visit Blythe. It was only then that the latter heard any of the details of the Rising.

In July, Blythe was moved to Reading Jail, where the British authorities sent those Irish prisoners whom they considered posed the greatest threat to the status quo in Ireland. About thirty or thirty-five men were selected from several other prisons, including some from Frongoch. Like many of the witnesses, Blythe was given to making lists. His list of prisoners in Reading Jail includes many familiar names. Sean T. O'Kelly, Ginger O'Connell, Denis McCullough and Pierce McCann were all well known to Blythe and to each other; Arthur Griffith was the principal figure amongst the prisoners, according to Blythe. Apart from the cultural activities run by Griffith – and respectfully described by Blythe – life in Reading settled down to something very similar to that in Frongoch, as described by Thomas Leahy. Ginger O'Connell ran military classes, classes in Irish were held, and there was a great deal of political discussion and planning the future. The prisoners even had parties, which Blythe remembers with pleasure:

> As most of us had a few pounds when arrested and as we were paid about a pound a week in the name of two or three prisoners who were supposed to be orderlies for keeping the place clean – all prisoners taking their turn at the actual work – we were always able to get extra sugar and butter, and also materials for the so-called birthday parties which we had every Sunday night. At these 'birthday parties' there was generally tea, ham, bread, butter, coffee and a few drinks for those who [drank]. Everybody who had money took his turn to give a 'birthday party'.

When the time came for the Reading prisoners to be released, there were different orders relating to Blythe. He found that the order by which he had been banished to England two weeks before the Rising was still in force. He seems to have been free to go anywhere he wanted in England; he was given a ticket to London, whereas the others were given tickets to Dublin. But Blythe went to Dublin anyway and eventually resumed his old career of recruiting for the Volunteers – beginning in Limerick, where he had been staying with the Daly family (Tom Clarke's wife's people).

Opinions among the nationalists who gave witness statements on life in the English prisons varied. James Foran, for instance, thought that nothing much had happened in Knutsford. Frank Robbins would not have agreed with him. As was his wont, Robbins describes life in Knutsford in some detail. The Morse code that he and others had learnt in the Citizen Army proved to be invaluable in relieving the long silence imposed on the Irish prisoners at the beginning of their time in Knutsford. They had to improvise, of course, and it was hard on the hands when they had to scrape on the walls to make the 'dash'. But Robbins managed to teach the code to a prisoner, a man named Tuke, who had not learned it before his stay in Knutsford ended, and by this means enlarged the conversational circle.

Tom Byrne might have had an easier time of it if he had been captured and served his time with the many other like-minded men who had been sent to English prisons. There was, however, the very real possibility of execution for Byrne. His rank in the Volunteers and his record in the Boer War (fighting on the side of the Boers) put him in real danger. So he went on the run. He had stayed in Liffey Street, very close to where he had been fighting for a couple of days. On Sunday, he and the other men decided to move. 'The only thing that looked respectable about me was my shoes', he recounts in his statement. (Byrne's old shoes had worn out on the long march from Kildare, and he had been given a new pair.) People were going to Mass when he made his move. He tried to get to Dorset Street via Henry Street and Upper Liffey Street, but the way was blocked by a British checkpoint.

He then went back to Abbey Street and into O'Connell Street, slouching along to avoid notice: he was well known to the police. He passed the Post Office, hoping to get to the Rotunda, but that way was cut off too. He crossed the street and at Findlater Place turned and made his way round the back of the Gresham Hotel to the rear of the Pro-Cathedral. Sitting on the steps of the Pro-Cathedral were some young fellows from the North, members of Edward Carson's Volunteers. Byrne and his comrade had no difficulty passing themselves off as harmless citizens. He recalls:

> We talked to them for a while about the deplorable state of affairs. I had a plug of hard tobacco and gave pieces to some of these fellows. Then I slouched by them and around the corner to the front of the Cathedral.

When he had got to Mountjoy Square by 'unfrequented routes', he was able to get a message to his mother, who rented a room in Eccles Street. That night, Byrne was able to call on her. His aunt had come over from Phibsboro with a good suit of clothes for him, and he stayed there that night. He would have stayed another night, but when he came back, the man who was renting out the rooms turned him away. He decided to visit:

> the lady who later became my wife. I went along to Eccles Street and turned into Nelson Street. I put on a brave front – I believe I looked like a detective – I crossed without interrogation into Mountjoy Street. I went up Palmerston Place to No. 1, where this lady lived with her mother and brother. She had been in the Post Office herself and went out with the wounded to Jervis Street Hospital. I had given her my watch and some money to mind for me.

He registered under a false name at a nearby hotel, where he stayed for two nights. When he began to feel uneasy, he moved for a couple of days with a friend. At last, he got to Baldoyle, where he was able to borrow a bicycle. With the bike, he was able to reach Balbriggan, where an old comrade of his called Joe Kennedy lived. The two men had soldiered together in the Irish Brigade in South Africa. Byrne stayed there for a few weeks. From there, he went to Stamullen in County Meath, where he stayed with a friend named Dardis. Moving ever northwards, Byrne was trying to reach his aunt and cousin's place near Carrickmacross. When he reached the farm he found that the RIC were occupying a hut right next it, so on he went. As he left one place, he was always given the name of people who would put him up at his next stop.

He eventually arrived in Derry and stayed a few weeks there before travelling on to Belfast. He felt it to be safe enough to travel part of the way by train. There he found another cousin, who ran 'a spirit grocery business', Byrne recalls, and stayed with him for several months, helping him in the business.

Just before Christmas, the British promised that there would be no more executions, and Byrne returned to Dublin. The nationalist movement had restarted and, like the men coming out of the English prisons, he had work to do. Besides, the unnamed 'young lady' who was to become his wife lived in Dublin. They got married in 1919 and set up home together in Eccles Street. He was arrested in 1920 just after the couple's first baby was born. If it had not been for the birth of the child, he would not have been home.

Of the four men who feature in this chapter, only one, Thomas Leahy, never worked in Ireland after the Treaty – which he opposed. Ernest Blythe became a member of the Provisional Government and went on to become director of the Abbey Theatre. Thomas Byrne became Captain of the Guard at Dáil Éireann after Michael Collins had put his name forward. Frank Robbins became General Secretary of the ITGWU.

Towards the end of his witness statement, Byrne tentatively suggests a reason why Collins might have put his name up for the job of Captain of the Guard, which he held until his retirement:

> As a matter of fact, I left the battalion at the request of Michael Collins. I know it is a fact that it was owing to the failure of the 1st Battalion to carry out certain operations on Bloody Sunday. In any case, he thought perhaps that Paddy Houlihan would be a better man. We held a meeting which was attended by Brigadier Oscar Traynor. He told me that at the request of Michael Collins, Houlihan took my place. The battalion officers did not want me to resign but I told them to obey GHQ [General Headquarters]. At any rate, whether he, Collins, thought he might have done me an injustice or not, it was he put my name forward for the job I later held in Leinster House.

As for the women who were so closely connected with the Rising and left witness statements, it should come as no surprise that they remained as active as ever.

While still in Mountjoy Jail, Dr Lynn and her friends began to attract a certain kind of media interest. Some American press representatives came to interview them. Dr Lynn recalls:

> We were brought into a room and were asked all sorts of questions. I remember there was a lady among them who

189

asked us were we 'diehards'. At that time I did not know what 'diehards' meant. She said afterwards that she never came across such a stupid set as we were. I think our brains were comatose after what we had been through and they refused to work for us. We were not at all up to the mark and as snappy as they would have liked us to be. They got the impression that we were a poor lot.

After her stay in Mountjoy, Dr Lynn was deported to England, into the charge of 'some friend of a friend' of her family. She managed to elude the friend, keeping the police happy and doing a little medical practice as a locum as well. It was not a happy time for her but she managed to get back to Dublin by August. She was there well in time to, she recounts, 'make great preparations for sending parcels to Frongoch. . . . Then suddenly the prisoners were all released.'

Dr Lynn was probably at the Sinn Féin Convention in the spring of 1917:

Whenever Sinn Féin started again, I was in it.

Mairín Cregan, from Killorglin, eventually boarded a train in Mallow and found again some of her former fellow-travellers:

especially two ladies who were returning from a holiday in Killarney. But though they had previously tried to make me one of their party, they now studiously avoided me, making remarks like 'She is one of them'; 'Did you ever see such lunacy, daring to fight the British Empire'; etc.

By the time she reached Dublin, the executions had begun. Her friends had not yet returned to Dublin, but her landlady welcomed her with open arms. She had guessed that Cregan had been involved with the movement and she, with great foresight, had checked her belongings for anything that might be construed as incriminating in the event of a police raid. She remembers that:

So many people were in jail or internment camps that it was not easy to get in touch with one's friends quickly. But eventually we got together again (those who left of our particular group) in Ryans', 19 Ranclagh Road – three members of their family were now absent in jails, as well as most of the people who used to foregather there on Sunday evenings.

Min Ryan was able to give her the memento – a coin with his initials scratched on it – which Sean McDermott had wanted her to have, because she had been "'a good girl" and had carried out my mission to Kerry in accordance with his instructions.'

In the weeks and months which followed, Cregan and her friends spent most of their time visiting fails and sending parcels to the prisoners, as well working for the Prisoners Dependents' Fund, an organisation which looked after prisoners' families.

In September 1916, Cregan left Dublin for Ballyshannon in Donegal, where she took up a temporary post in the convent school. She had been dismissed from her teaching post in St Louis Convent in Rathmines as a result of her involvement with the Volunteers. She recalls that:

Some of the parents of the children were calling to the Reverend Mother, protesting against their children being taught by a friend of 'those rebels', and who herself was strongly suspected of having been mixed up in 'this rebellion'.

In September 1917, she got a teaching job with the Dominican Sisters in Portstewart, County Antrim, where she remained until 1919, when she married Dr Jim Ryan.

Slowly, attitudes towards the 'rebels' were changing. Just one month after the execution of Thomas MacDonagh, Eileen McGrane, a student of MacDonagh's who had had no connection with the movement before the Rising, set about having a month's mind Mass said for him in University Church in Dublin. McGrane remembers:

We put a notice in the paper and the Mass was attended by many others outside the student circles, including Rory O'Connor. The notice we sent to the papers included a verse about MacDonagh's having died for his country, but that part was omitted.

Shortly afterwards, McGrane joined the Central Branch of Cuman na mBan. Her efforts to start a branch in UCD failed, however. The executive of Cumann ne mBan disapproved of the idea, 'thinking we just wanted to be exclusive', according to McGrane.

They were permitted, however, to form a 'half-branch' of Inghinidhe na hÉireann 'with our own officer with the rank of Lieutenant.'

15

FROM THE OTHER SIDE

In April 1916, Captain E. Gerrard, an officer in the British army, came home from the Dardanelles and was stationed at Athlone. He was a past pupil of Clongowes Wood College, as indeed was his fellow officer John O'Beirne, 'one of the O'Beirnes of Roscommon,' the former states. Captain Gerrard opens his witness statement with a telling anecdote:

> About the 18th July 1914, when I was 2nd Lieutenant, Glen Imaal Practice Camp, I rode down with Major Haig – at that time second-in-command of the King's Own Scottish Borderers – I said to him casually – we were both on horses – 'What a lovely country. I hope you will like it.' He said, 'I hate the —ing place. I hate the —ing people.' Major Haig was in command of the Company of the King's Own Scottish Borderers, who opened fire on civilians at Bachelor's Walk a few days later. I often wondered was there any connection between what he said to me and his action. He was always known in the British army afterwards as 'the man who made the war'.

Captain Gerrard remembered well the events of the Rising, insofar as they affected him and his men. We are fortunate that he availed himself of the opportunity to give a witness statement to the Bureau when the Rising was over and everything was calm again. At the very least, Athlone could not be said to have been in a state of battle-readiness in 1916. Captain Gerrard recalls:

In Athlone there were two batteries – eight guns. Not one of these guns was in a position to fire without being oiled and pumped by the artificers. It would have taken them two days to get them into action. The only ammunition of any sort in Athlone was shrapnel. There was no high explosive, no smoke, and no incendiary shells. I know that for a fact.

Captain Gerrard denied the allegation that the British fired incendiary shells in Dublin, as 'Both batteries were commanded by two men who were unable to ride a horse.' It seems that the man who was second-in-command of the guns – and who weighed more than twenty-five stone – was, according to Captain Gerrard, 'the most incompetent Captain of the whole British army.'

In Athlone, the British managed to make fit for action four guns out of the eight; these four guns were then brought up to Dublin by train. Captain Gerrard would have been given the job of getting the guns to Dublin if he had not been on leave – at home in Dublin. He tells a story which must have done the rounds for years:

> The Acting Captain doing 'Q' side was Lieutenant C. H. Dickens. He told me that he had a shot at the flag on top of the GPO with one of these guns. He did not realise that the shell would not burst. The shell travelled on to the lawn of the Vice-Regal Lodge. He told me that the Lord Lieutenant was very annoyed at being shelled.

Captain Gerrard was one of those curious citizens who went into Dublin to see what was going on at the beginning of the week:

> I saw the insurrection troops assembling at the top of Grafton Street and going into Stephen's Green. I was specially struck with their magnificent physique. They were huge men. I realised there was something serious going on, and I went home and got my uniform in a bag. When going home, I met Sir Frederick Shaw, Bushy Park, and he told me to go into Beggars Bush Barracks.

The garrison in Beggars Bush was hopelessly undermanned until the Sherwood Foresters, a regiment of the British army, arrived later in the week. For three days, only Sir Frederick Shaw, Captain Gerrard, one or two other officers, four non-commissioned officers and about ten men were holding the barracks. Captain Gerrard remembers:

I was the only officer there who had seen a shot fired of any sort, except Sir Frederick Shaw. He told me that he had been in arms against the Fenians when he was in the Life Guards in 1867 at the Battle of Tallaght.

Such was the relentless continuity of Irish history.

Captain Gerrard relates a little-known tragedy from the engagement in Beggars Bush:

One of my sentries in Beggars Bush Barracks, about Tuesday evening, said to me, 'I beg your pardon, sir, I have just shot two girls.' I said, 'What on earth did you do that for?' He said, 'I thought they were rebels. I was told they were dressed in all classes of attire.' At a range of about two hundred yards I saw two girls – about twenty [years old] – lying dead.

When the Sherwood Foresters arrived on Wednesday, a continuous stream of rifle fire was directed towards the positions held by the Volunteers. Captain Gerrard complained of the quality of the Sherwood Foresters:

The young Sherwoods that I had with me had never fired a service rifle before. They were not even able to load them. We had to show them how to load them.

He described these recruits as 'untrained, undersized products of the English slums.'

On Wednesday, Captain Gerrard led a party in an attempt to get to grips with the 'Sinn Féiners':

As soon as I got over the wall, at a range of about 200 yards, about eight Sinn Féiners advanced from the direction of the city to meet us. I saw them coming towards us firing. There was what they call a fairly sharp firefight. These men were standing up, not lying down. They came out of their trenches to meet us. They were very brave, I remember.

The Captain's statement is an eloquent testimony to the high regard in which a British officer of his day could hold a soldier, be he enemy or friend, if he possessed the virtue of courage.

There is another witness statement in the archives of the Bureau of Military History made by a member of the British army: one Maurice Meade. His background was somewhat different from that of Captain Gerrard. Meade relates that he:

> was born on the 11th May 1893, at Ballinavana, Elton, County Limerick. There was a big family of us in it and, having gone to school to the local national school until I was twelve years of age, I had then to leave school and go to work with a local farmer. All my pay was taken up by my father to help in keeping the family, so that I never saw a halfpenny of what I earned. My father kept me fed and clothed but I never had the spending of any money. I had no interest in, nor did I know anything of, the national movement at the time. My time was fully occupied in helping to make ends meet.

By the time he was seventeen, Meade had made up his mind to join the British army. He tells us that he chose this way of life in order to gain some personal – and economic – independence. Although this was of course part of the reason, to judge from the amazing tale he tells in his witness statement, a love of adventure – as well as the companionship of his comrades – was a large portion of the attraction he felt towards army life. He was clearly delighted when his talent for running was noticed, shortly after he enlisted.

Meade had already enlisted when John Redmond made his extraordinary speech at Woodenbridge and Westminster calling on the Volunteers to join the British army to fight for Belgium's independence. Some people did not take kindly to the role that the Irish Parliamentary Party had taken upon itself – that of recruiting sergeant for the British army – and recruitment for the British army never reached the level that Redmond would have wished. As the war progressed and the number of casualties rose, whatever enthusiasm there had been among the Irish for the war in the early months of the conflict ebbed away. The shadow of the threat of conscription added to anti-war feelings. In the long run, if anything the First World War deepened the divisions between Catholics and Protestants. The blood that was spilt so prodigally in the battles of that terrible war bound the Protestants of the North more closely to the British Crown and the British Empire. For the Catholics, the blood sacrifice of their young men on the same battlefields of Europe was a waste and a terrible sadness; the Protestants regarded their involvement in the war as a badge of honour.

But that was to be in the future. One of our most charming witnesses, Aguistin MacGiolla Iosa (or, in its original form, Augustine Ingoldsby) tells us a story about his brother-in-law William Breen. Breen, an electrical engineer, was in charge of the electrical department in the well-known Dublin hardware store Dockrell's. Breen joined the Volunteers and became a Captain, and he was interned for his part in the Rising. MacGiolla Iosa recalls:

> When he [William Breen] came back to Dockrell's after his internment, he went to work and the heads of the various departments and other employees went as a deputation to Sir Maurice Dockrell and told him they would not continue to work in the same firm as Breen. Sir Maurice said Breen fought according to his colour and they themselves were able-bodied men who should be in khaki fighting at the front, and if they did not want to work in the same firm as Breen, they knew their way out.

Sir Maurice spoke for us all. All the men and women lived and died according to their colour. As did those others who lived according to another colour.

16

'THIS LAMENTABLE DISTURBANCE'

The years immediately before and after 1916 were ones of intense soul-searching in Catholic and nationalist circles. It was not easy even for those people who were closely involved in the political events of the day to endure the censure of their church but at least they knew where they stood. People at one remove from these affairs, such as family members, must have been confused. Those IRB members who were Catholics had to reckon with the Catholic Church's condemnation of an oath-bound secret society whose ultimate aim was to establish a free Republic. But the hostility of the Church was not confined to the IRB. The anti-republican stance of the Church had deep roots in Catholic history, and owed as much to the relationship of the Pope and the Vatican to Italian nationalism in the nineteenth century as to the activities of the Fenians. Moreover, during the nineteenth century, the Catholic Church in Ireland had learned to live with English domination and English civilisation in Britain. This tension between some nationalist families and the Church lasted from the mid-nineteenth century right up to 1916 and beyond. Seamus Robinson thought this issue important enough to include an account of his own family history in his witness statement. He asserts:

> All this may not be history in the ordinary sense, but history cannot be properly understood without some appreciation of all that went to make up the psychology of the people at any given time.

Robinson goes back to his great-grandfather to explain certain aspects of his family's attitude towards the Church. His great-grandfather had not been a Catholic; in fact, he had been a Grand Master of the Orange Lodge and had married a 'saintly Catholic woman', Robinson reports. Although he did not like to see his sons being brought up as Catholics, his son, Seamus's grandfather, was indeed a Catholic. Seamus's grandfather accepted the Church's ruling on the Fenians: the bishops had the power to excommunicate. Nonetheless, he strongly resented the ruling, and went so far as to say that the bishops were morally wrong. There was a family belief that their Protestant forebear had connections with the 1798 Rising too.

Seamus Robinson describes his own parents as typical Catholic nationalists of their day:

Their sympathy was with Parnell but they couldn't take sides against the bishops. They had also become convinced that the British Empire was invincible. They had all the arguments against us young people. Then the '98 centenary celebrations set us youngsters agog and enquiring. We wanted to prepare for another fight but we were told not to be foolish. 'It would be lovely if it could be done,' we were told, 'but your grandfathers failed and your great-grandfathers failed, all better men than you could ever hope to be, and besides England has become much stronger and is just as ruthless.' I think it was Joe, my brother, who first pointed out to me that we should be ashamed of our father's generation. They were the first generation of Irishmen who had not struck a blow for Ireland.

The attitude to Irish nationalism of the Irish bishops, which in Robinson's words 'hung like a pall over every generous impulse to free our country', worried so many young recruits to the IRB that in 1909 or 1910 the leaders decided to do something about it. They called a meeting. Ernest Blythe, who was nineteen or twenty at the time, remembered it very well:

I was in Dublin. The main activity was simply recruiting. The most outstanding thing I remember was a kind of mass meeting held in the Clontarf Town Hall. Several members of the organisation apparently had had conscientious scruples and had mentioned the fact of their membership in Confession, with the result that the priests had told them they were to get out. Consequently a number of members were lost. The authorities of the organisation in Dublin thought of a way to stop it.

When suddenly one Sunday afternoon I was mobilised for the meeting in the Clontarf Town Hall that night, I was told that it was to hear a statement by a priest who was himself a member of the organisation. I saw a lot of people in the hall whom I was astonished to learn were members. For example, Jack Shouldice, who was over me in the Department of Agriculture and whom I had never suspected of being in the IRB. The priest was Father O'Sullivan (a brother, I heard afterwards, of Diarmuid Ó Duibhne), who was on a mission to America. He was a member, I gathered afterwards, of Clan na Gael and not exactly a member of the IRB. I looked forward with some interest to hearing why he felt that the IRB did not come under the classification of a condemned secret society. He did not touch on the point at all, but merely said he was a member, that he had no conscientious troubles, and proceeded to make a patriotic speech. The meeting, however, was quite effective, because we heard nothing more of members leaving for some time.

To say that the news of the Rising was unwelcome to the Church authorities would be an understatement. Cardinal Logue, who in 1916 was the Primate of Ireland and Archbishop of Armagh, set out the situation very clearly in his address to the assembled priests of the Maynooth Union at its general meeting in 1916. His first concern was that the priests were going to get the blame for the 'late lamentable occurrences'. It was, he said, his experience that that was what usually happened: 'Whatever went wrong, the first thing the governors of the country and the administrators turned to was to heap the blame upon the priesthood.'

Cardinal Logue had no intention of allowing this to happen during his Primacy. In the course of his address, he named the associations which had attracted the suspicions of the authorities, and with which some priests might be connected. The Gaelic League was one such. It was quite unjust for him to regard members of the Gaelic League as Sinn Féiners: he himself had been very enthusiastic about the League and he was no Sinn Féiner. Another example that the Cardinal cited was the various bodies of the Volunteers. He himself had never been enthusiastic about the Volunteers but he stated that 'it does not at all follow from the fact that a person who sympathised with, or attended meetings of, the Volunteers was disloyal or had any designs against the government or the authorities of the country. I believe that not one in five hundred of them ever foresaw what any inner body was driving at – the organisation of a rebellion, a foolish and absurd insurrection of the people of the country.'

Cardinal Logue's first thought when he heard on Easter Monday of what he described as 'this foolish and pernicious insurrection' was that 'the Public Authorities will muddle this, as sure as the sun shines': in his opinion, they surely did. The cardinal took no issue with the authorities for defending the rights of the State but noted that 'they sent out emissaries and picked every man who belonged to the Irish Volunteers. . . . I think that was the greatest act of folly any government could have been guilty of. They should have let this die out like a bad dream – and it was a dream, so painful that it was unlikely to be repeated.'

Towards the end of his address, Cardinal Logue set out his own dream for Ireland. Irishmen should love their country and their religion, he thought, but this attachment should not stand between them and their duty to the higher power. On the contrary, they had the strongest proofs that 'when, unfortunately, this lamentable disturbance arose, the Irish were rallying round the State and the Empire and sending their best and dearest to shed their blood on the battlefields of Europe and Asia.'

The Cardinal was all set to bask in what he regarded as this new-found unity. According to the record of the General Meeting of the Maynooth Union in 1916:

201

'I thought that would have put an end,' said his Eminence, 'to any little jealousy or heart-burning that existed between the different parts of the Empire – between England and Scotland and Ireland. Unfortunately the whole thing is knocked up now.'

There is no doubt that the Rising 'knocked up' the Cardinal's vision for Ireland. Indeed, well before the Rising, the pervasive propaganda of the British establishment in war mode was beginning to get on the nerves of even quite moderate people. Father Eugene Nevin, the Passionist Father from Mount Argus, does his best in his statement to describe the intense feelings aroused by the war, and the recruitment effort relating to it. He found it hard to take the waving Union Jacks and the singing of 'God Save the King'. Such was the effect of the war fever and the propaganda that, according to Father Nevin, many Irish nationalists lost hope in the future of their country:

> There were few families among the working class in Dublin at that time that were not in some way connected with the English army, having a son, a brother in it. The same might be said of the large towns where soldiers' barracks were located, the result being that there was a strong pro-English and anti-German feeling throughout the country.

The competition for recruits was fierce, from the Volunteers on the one hand and the British army on the other. Father Nevin reports in his witness statement that, when the leader of the Irish Parliamentary Party, John Redmond, in the course of a stirring House of Commons speech, made his offer of the use of the Volunteers in the war effort:

> a pro-British feeling like a huge wave of the sea swept over the whole country, leaving but a few dry places as foothold for those fortunate to escape an inundation that threatened to engulf the Church.

Father Nevin and others like him found it difficult to accept that people who hitherto would not have dreamed of even mentioning the advantages of joining the British army now seemed to be considering enlisting. He witnessed an instance of this shift in attitudes while on a sick call. The doctor who was on the same sick call was, in Father Nevin's opinion, 'becoming an English recruiting sergeant.' But when the clergy began to act in the same way, it is hard to imagine his dismay. He recalls:

It was deplorable, disconcerting and bewildering to the young men and the country in general to see their Reverend, their Very Reverend and Right Reverend fathers in God, hobnobbing with British recruiting agents. Aye! On the platform with MPs and a Cabinet minister who openly declared: 'We make no bones about it, we have come over to get your young men for our army.' That was the situation confronting us in 1915: and while highly poised clergymen in the secular order – the higher Superiors among the Regulars, backed by a mercenary press – were orating up and down the country on behalf of England, for an ordinary cleric to hold and maintain a contrary opinion and course was little short of a misdemeanour.

These sentiments were far removed from those expressed by Cardinal Logue when, on the conclusion of his address to the priests at Maynooth, he wished that no obstacle should exist 'between the members of our Irish nation here and other parts of the Empire'.

Even Cardinal Logue found it hard to swallow some aspects of British policy, especially in the field of education. He was deeply hurt by the school books imposed on the system, which were designed to turn Irish children into what the educationalist 'Dr Whately wanted them to be, "happy English children".'

Priests who were sympathetic to the nationalist cause became well known to the Volunteers. They were often adopted by them as unofficial chaplains and were sought out for the hearing of Confessions. Father Nevin took great pleasure in agreeing to celebrate a special Mass for the 4th Battalion of the Irish Volunteers – for which they had arranged a military parade. His sermon on that occasion was later published. In his witness statement, Father Nevin writes:

When at the customary time I had read the weekly notices, standing behind the altar rails, I closed the book and addressed them. I learned afterwards that many of them were very apprehensive of what they were going to get, denunciation or what? But I soon set them at ease, and, as they told me afterwards, they felt walking on air all that day, it being the first church approval they had received. . . . The year was 1916.

Long before 1916, and indeed long afterward, it was not unusual for Catholic priests to be passionately interested in politics. Indeed, a smaller number, particularly some curates, were members of Sinn Féin. Some supported the volunteers of either variety (the Irish Volunteers or Redmond's National Volunteers). There must, however, have been very few of the calibre of the Reverend Eugene Canon Coyle PP of Devenish, County Fermanagh. In 1914, Father Coyle, as he was then, was curate in Fintona, County Tyrone. Fintona was, in the words of Canon Coyle, 'a Catholic town'. The balance of power between Protestant and Catholic changed when the Ulster Volunteers armed themselves. To make matters worse, when the Redmondite Volunteers split off from the Sinn Féin section, Father Coyle became worried, particularly as the 'Ulster Volunteers were well organised in Fintona and paraded the town carrying arms two or three times a week.' The small group of Fintona Volunteers, unarmed as they were, felt distinctly vulnerable. Father Coyle decided that the time had come for him to take steps to restore the balance of power somewhat. He recalls:

> I went to Dublin and called on The O'Rahilly and explained to him my people's situation in Fintona and my determination to help, so far as I could possibly do it, in getting our people armed. I gave him a cheque out of my private means, which at that time were limited, for £150 for rifles for my parishioners. He supplied me with sixty rifles, a bayonet for each rifle and a supply of suitable ammunition. Those rifles etc were packed into cases and were put on the train. I returned from Dublin and all arrived safely in Fintona.

Nobody interfered with the freight on the train, and it was unloaded without incident. A few nights later, Father Coyle was able to dispose of the sixty rifles and bayonets, together with the ammunition, to the Fintona Volunteers at the price he had paid for them. He continues:

Shortly after this, sixty young Fintona Volunteers paraded on the streets of our town, all armed with serviceable rifles, each rifle having attached a fixed bayonet.

At the time, the Ulster Volunteers in Fintona had no bayonets. Following Canon Coyle's intervention, the intimidating parades through Fintona by the Ulster Volunteers became far less frequent.

Canon Coyle was one of the very few priests who addressed the thorny question of their relationship with the IRB:

In the peculiar situation of our Irish people in those early years of 1914–15, I believed that defensive military preparation by our people was the keystone of our national well-being. I attended with Dr McCartan all the principal meetings of the IRB in County Tyrone. I was not an official member of the organisation; my priestly calling would not allow my joining an oath-bound secret society. I attended those meetings, and in this way I hoped to give the country boys the feeling that they were working on the right lines by organising, arming and training for the defence of our country.

Canon Coyle became a great friend of Dr McCartan in the years before the Rising. They worked hard on recruiting for the Volunteers and in the procuring of arms and the training of the men. The Canon was usually accompanied by another priest, Father (later Canon) James Daly, when he attended IRB meetings in County Tyrone. The Bureau of Military History persuaded Father Daly to give a witness statement, which he would write himself. Although Canon Daly made no effort to deny his membership of the Brotherhood, he was a reluctant witness: when the man from the Bureau returned, he found that Canon Daly had written nothing. When the man from the Bureau returned the next day, however, the canon had some notes written. Between them – and at the Canon's dictation – the two men put the witness statement together. On the cover page of the statement, with the full consent of the witness, his identity is written: 'Very Rev James Canon O'Daly PP Clogher, County Tyrone. Member of the IRB; Confidant of Irish Volunteers.'

Ernest Blythe, who, as a Protestant, was a disengaged observer, was extremely interested in the situation of Catholic nationalists and their relationships with their clergy. He had noticed that Sean McDermott appeared to have sufficient friends amongst the clergy for his purpose of promoting the interests of the IRB. When Blythe was about to be arrested under the Defence of the Realm Act for his recruiting activities, these contacts came in useful. Blythe decided not to give himself up; instead, he went to Dublin for advice. On arrival in Dublin, he recalls that he went:

> to the offices of the *Scissors and Paste,* or whatever the paper was called at the time, in D'Olier Street. There I met Sean McDermott and Arthur Griffith, both of whom agreed entirely with what I had decided on. However, Griffith suggested that it would be a good thing from the propagandist point of view if I could be arrested in the house of a parish priest. I told him that I did not know any parish priest whom I could ask to take me in, that up till then all the help I had got in organising the Volunteers had been from curates, and that so far, no parish priest had shown any sympathy.

But Griffith knew a parish priest in County Monaghan who, he felt sure, would be glad to put Blythe up and make all the proper outraged noises when Blythe was duly arrested. Everything was arranged within a few days. Blythe went off to Monaghan to be arrested by the RIC. He was somewhat deflated when the police seemed to have lost him and was reduced to writing as many postcards as he could to his friends, on which he gave details of his whereabouts. Shortly afterwards, he was duly arrested.

Sean McDermott's contacts were spread far and wide. When Patrick O'Daly, who had joined the IRB in 1907, left Dublin to work in Galway sometime in 1913, he became a member of the IRB in Tuam. O'Daly left Dublin armed with a letter of introduction from McDermott, to be given to George Nichols, the Head Centre in Galway. O'Daly recalls that, when he arrived in Tuam, the Circle was almost broken up:

> When I was leaving Dublin Sean McDermott told me about this and asked me to get in touch with a Father Foley, a very old man and a Jesuit Father, who was then in Salthill [in County Galway]. This Jesuit was very intimate with Sean McDermott, and when I contacted him I found [him to be] a strong believer in the IRB, and he gave me every encouragement regarding the organisation. He told me to have nothing to do with the lukewarm members and thought a great deal of George Nichols.

It is unlikely that many members of religious orders were also IRB men. Sympathetic priests were known to the IRB, however. Tom Harris was not surprised when his small band of revolutionaries from Kildare were told to collect their gelignite from the Dominican College in Newbridge, where it was being looked after by a Father McCluskey, who was sympathetic and, Harris remembers, 'probably in the know'.

17

THE CASTLE DOCUMENT

AND OTHER CONTROVERSIES

In a sense, each of the witness statements is an attempt to set the record straight, but there are some which would not have been made at all if the witness had not believed strongly at the time the evidence was being collected that, if they neglected to give their statement, the truth, as they saw it, might be lost forever. The witness statements regarding the 'Castle Document', as it came to be known, was one such. The leaked document, which caused consternation when it was published on Spy Wednesday 1916, has been the subject of controversy ever since.

The document, which was said to have been purloined from the Secretary's Office in Dublin Castle, gave detailed instructions to the police and military regarding the proposed arrest of many important and well-known public men and the raiding of the homes and residences of certain other people, all distinguished in the city, including the Archbishop of Dublin, Dr William Walsh. The attention this document attracted in the decade 1947–57, and even today, is far greater than it attracted in 1916. The provenance of the document affected the credibility of several still-loved participants in the Rising.

Grace Plunkett, who married Joe Plunkett in Kilmainham Jail on the day before his execution, refers to the document. So does her brother-in-law Jack Plunkett, in his statement. Min Ryan, later Mrs Richard Mulcahy, did not believe it was authentic. She notes in her statement that:

A great many of us held that it was not an authentic document. Some say Joe Plunkett wrote it.

The manner of publication of the Castle Document ensured maximum publicity for it. Alderman Tom Kelly read out the document to a meeting of the Dublin Corporation on 19 April 1916. Sean T. O'Kelly, who was President of Ireland when he gave his testimony in 1953, thinks this must have been a special meeting, called perhaps to decide on the rate of local taxation for the coming financial year. The contents of the document were explosive. That evening, the papers published the document in full under huge headlines.

Alderman Kelly was highly regarded by all parties, and anything he said was taken very seriously. The fact that he believed the document was genuine went a long way to convincing the public that this was indeed the case.

As soon as the initial reaction of shock and anger had begun to fade, the pro-British establishment and members of the Irish Parliamentary Party pooh-poohed the document. In their view, the whole thing was a complete fabrication, put together by extremists. They accepted whatever the Chief Secretary's Office told them about their enquiries into the document: 'No such document ever existed in the Chief Secretary's Office.' The office further stated that 'there was never any intention to arrest the people mentioned in the document, and most certainly not to raid the houses of the prominent people, including the Archbishop, whose names were given in the document.'

It was not only the pro-British establishment in Dublin that was too ready to believe that the document was bogus. Long after the events surrounding the affair had been virtually forgotten, apologists for Eoin MacNeill found yet another explanation for his efforts to cancel the Rising at the last minute. There are other explanations for MacNeill's action, which do him no dishonour.

It seems that the existence of Witness Statement 334, which was submitted to the Bureau by Eugene Smith, is of no small importance in the context of verifying the provenance of the Castle Document, if for no other reason than that we owe Grace Plunkett and Sean McDermott the dignity of listening to what they have to say on the subject. Smith at the time lived in Bird Avenue in Dundrum, Dublin. His identity is given as 'Official in Dublin Castle, the transfer of information to iv, 1913–1916.' Smith's evidence is worth reproducing at some length:

1   Before the Rising I was an official in the Castle and in that capacity a certain document came into my hands. It was a long communication from Major General Friend, General Officer Commanding the Forces in Ireland, and addressed to the Chief Secretary in London. I believed at the time, and still believe, that it was sent in reply to a query as to what military precautions would be necessary with a view to the enforcement of conscription in Ireland. The document was not in code or cipher.

2   It was unusual for Major General Friend to send communications from the Castle to London, as he had a private line from his headquarters at Kilmainham to London. It may have been that the matter dealt with in the document was discussed with Sir Mathew Nathan at the Castle and that was the reason the communication was sent from there, or it may have been that the private line connected only with military headquarters in London and not with the Chief Secretary's Office.

3   It was a lengthy document – about the length of that published in the press; but I had ample time to study the details of it, as it was I dealt with it, and I memorised the main points of it. I was deeply interested in the political situation in Ireland and in the threat of the application of conscription to Ireland, which was then, to the best of my recollection, under consideration in the British press and in the House of Commons.

Smith did not feel bound by the oath of secrecy which, as an official of the Castle, he had taken, and he decided to pass on this information to 'those whom it concerned'. By this, he may have meant the IRB. His contacts included some names that feature in

210

other witness statements, including Jack Shouldice, Paddy Sheahan and Maurice Collins. The contents of the document which Smith passed on were practically identical to those of the document read out at the Corporation meeting by Alderman Kelly, 'except that,' Smith recalls, 'so far as I can recollect, it did not state that the operations suggested by Major General Friend were authorised by the Chief Secretary, and there was no reference to maps or lists. The words "Ara Coeli" were mentioned as being the archbishop's house, and in this I think Major General Friend confused the Archbishop's Palace with that of Cardinal Logue.'

Be that as it may, it is certain that, if Joe Plunkett were to have forged this document, he would never have confused Armagh with Dublin, or the residences of the respective dignitaries of the Church.

Grace Plunkett recalls:

I remember the document that was published in Holy Week, because I wrote it out myself for Joe, sitting on the edge of his bed, in Larkfield House. Joe did not do it in the Nursing Home. Although it was published in Holy Week, it had come out from the Castle sometime before that. It did come out of the Castle. That is quite certain. I know who brought it. Donagh MacDonagh was married to a girl named Smith. It was her father who brought it out. Mr Smith was in the Castle. He now lives, I think, at Mayville, Bird Avenue, Dundrum.

In his witness statement, Jack Plunkett explains an aspect of the evidence given by Grace Plunkett about the publication of the document, that at first might be puzzling. He was convinced that the use of Morse code was to disguise 'the fact that the information had been obtained direct from somebody in the Castle, who was to be protected. I know that some document was printed at Larkfield in many hundreds.'

The strangest response to the claim that the document was authentic was that of Monsignor Patrick Browne, who, on 10 May, visited Sean McDermott in Kilmainham Jail – two days before his execution. The visit was meant to last half an hour but the officer in charge – Major Lennon – had forgotten that the priest was still there. As a result, it was 'in the small hours of the morning when I left,' Monsignor Browne recalls. 'I was about five or six hours there.' The priest and the condemned man talked about a wide variety of subjects, including the Castle Document. In his statement, Monsignor Browne remembers:

> Another thing he told me – and I don't know whether he was deceived about it or not – was about the document that was published in Paddy Little's paper and given out at the Corporation, about certain houses being cordoned off and leaders of the Volunteers to be arrested. He said that it was an absolutely genuine document. Although it was his last night on earth and he spoke with great conviction, I found great difficulty in believing it. That would have been about the most important item of our conversation, as far as history is concerned.

Simon Donnelly, as well as submitting narrative statements regarding his experiences in 1916 – he had been appointed officer Commanding C Company of the 3rd Battalion on Easter Monday, as the battalion was about to go into action – wrote a very careful letter to the Bureau of Military History, dated 21 April 1948. He composed this letter, he tells us, in order to prevent an incorrect record leading to historical error. The letter refers to an article published in the 10 April 1926 issue of *An t-Oglach*. The article, in the course of lauding the courage and skill of Donnelly, indirectly attacks Éamon de Valera's ability as the commandant of the 3rd Battalion at Bolands Mills in 1916. The reason for Donnelly's promotion was, as he put it, because:

> the captain had told Lieutenant Malone and myself on the previous Sunday that he would comply with MacNeill's countermanding order and not parade.

The man who wrote the article in *An t-Oglach* had also fought at Bolands Mills in 1916. His name was George A. Lyons. Donnelly took grave exception to one section of the article, especially the sentence:

He was a good second to de Valera and came very near supplanting him on one occasion.

In his statement, Donnelly puts the author of the article right:

Firstly – Throughout the entire week's fighting, Com. de
Valera enjoyed the fullest and sincerest loyalty of all ranks,
officers and men, without a single exception, and there
could not be any question of anyone supplanting him, least
of all myself, as, during the week's fighting, we were very
much together, and the greatest, in fact unbreakable, loyalty prevailed between the Commandant and myself. We were
all very attached to our Commandant. Latter-day politics
cannot alter or take from the loyalty and devotion to our
accepted leader during Easter Week, 1916.

Another question of great interest at the time the witness statements were recorded was whether Éamon de Valera had ever been
a member of the IRB. Sean Murphy (the resident caretaker at
Dublin Castle and an IRB man) does his best to illuminate the question, albeit with little success. Murphy recalls:

On that day I had a mission to carry out at No. 2 Dawson
Street, which was to introduce to Thomas MacDonagh,
Commandant Éamon de Valera, I previously having been
asked by Sean Tobin if I had any idea if de Valera was a
member of the IRB. I said as far as I knew he was not.

On the Tuesday Sean Tobin asked me could I speak to
de Valera and ask him to attend at No. 2 Dawson Street
with me on the Holy Thursday, which he did. I had mentioned to de Valera the matter of his becoming a member
of the IRB at the parade ground, Camden Row. We met at
No. 2 Dawson Street on Holy Thursday. I think it was as a
potential member of IRB that I introduced him to Thomas
MacDonagh, and they went into a private room. The result
of the interview or of what happened thereat I know not.

Frank Robbins made a very substantial contribution to the wit-
ness-statement archives, and he makes reasonable arguments to

justify a number of disputed events. For example, why did the insurgents not capture Dublin Castle (a question which was also raised by the playwright Sean O'Casey)? Robbins remembers:

> I can say authoritatively that it was never intended that the Irish Citizen Army should capture Dublin Castle. In the first instance, it would require many hundreds of men, as against our twenty-odd who took on the job of isolating Dublin Castle. Further to this, Mr William O'Brien informs me that some time before the Insurrection took place, James Connolly told him of the intention to isolate the Castle. William O'Brien felt disappointed at this information, and suggested to Connolly that, as Dublin Castle was known throughout the world as the stronghold of British imperialism in this country, if it was not the intention to capture it, why not burn it? Connolly informed William O'Brien that the suggestion of burning Dublin Castle was not practical, and pointed out that there was a Red Cross Hospital established in the Castle with approximately 500 wounded British soldiers. It was intended [to occupy] certain buildings commanding the entrance gates.

Secondly, why did the Volunteers occupy St Stephens Green – surely an act of suicide? Again, Robbins gives the answer: plans had to be changed at the last minute. According to the original plan, the Shelbourne Hotel was to be occupied by Lieutenant Norgrove, who was to have fifty men at his disposal. Such a force of men was not available, and Norgrove was detailed to the GPO instead. The women members cleared St Stephen's Green because there were no men available to do it. But the Citizen Army did hold the College of Surgeons until the surrender. Like many another participant, Robbins found it hard to take criticism from hurlers on the ditch: it is generally agreed that that is where the best hurlers are to be found.

CONCLUSION

Whether Frank Robbins knew it or not, the real value of the statements that he and others made does not lie in their power of vindication. Vindication has a certain importance, I suppose, for those who harbour a partisan view of the events of the 1916, but it is limited by the fact that these archives were locked up and out of reach for more than fifty years.

The value of the statements lies in their existence rather than merely in their content. The fact that in 1944 the editor of the armed forces' in-house magazine *An Cosantoir* was able to initiate the process of collecting and preserving the statements is in itself remarkable.

The origins of the work done by the Bureau of Military History go back to 1944, before the Bureau itself was established. The date is significant. The Second World War – a war in which the Irish State took up a position of wary neutrality – was about to enter its final year. Few dissented from this position of neutrality, and Taoiseach Éamon de Valera enjoyed unparalleled support throughout the war years. It was a time of great unity in the country. The war – or 'the emergency', as it came to be called – had a significant effect on life in Ireland. One consequence was that the Irish army was greatly expanded. In the book *The Irish Experinece During the Second World War: An Oral History,* Brigadier General Hogan tells the writer of the book, Benjamin Grob-FitzGibbon, that the Irish army, which had numbered only 5,000 when Hogan joined the Cadets in 1938, was completely 'unrepresentative'. He continues: 'The civil war was over fifteen or sixteen years before I joined, but still the leaders of the army and everyone above the rank of Lieutenant in it had fought in the civil war' (and on the winning side).

When it was clear that a second world war was imminent, men

who had fought on the other side in the civil war, or their sons, began to enlist in the armed forces. It was in the army that the rifts left by the civil war began to narrow. It thus became possible for de Valera to approve a plan put forward by Major Florence O'Donoghue. The Bureau of Military History, which was funded by the Department of Defence and largely staffed by army personnel, was entrusted with the task of collecting the witness statements, as well as contemporary documents, press cuttings, photographs and some voice recordings, from people who had been active in the 'national movement' between 1913 and 1921, more or less. When all the material had been collected, it was placed in the Military Archives for safe keeping.

It is highly probable that the people who were responsible for this enterprise were all too conscious of the paradox pointed out by Martin Mansergh in his paper 'The Uses of History', which is reproduced in his book *The Legacy of History*: 'The paradox is that people who live through a period will know many things that they take for granted, and will take their knowledge, not just their secrets, with them to the grave.' No doubt the motive for encouraging the participants to record their experiences of the years immediately before and after the 1916 Rising was the consciousness of time passing. The participants themselves may, I think, have had another motive. At the time the statements were taken down, the idea that telling one's 'story' might be good for one's psychological health was not widely proclaimed. 'Truth and reconciliation' commissions, such as the one established in South Africa after the demise of the apartheid system, were unknown. In many ways, these statements, which were confidential and guaranteed not to be looked at until everyone involved was safely dead, fulfil the function of such a commission. One might imagine that those who gave the statements would be talking to the people who came after them. In fact, I believe that they were more likely to be talking to themselves. We are privileged to be able to listen to them.

SUGGESTIONS FOR FURTHER READING

R. F. Foster, *Modern Ireland 1600–1912,* Allen Lane

Sinead McCoole, *No Ordinary Women,* O'Brien Press

Jim McDermott, *Northern Divisions,* Beyond the Pale Publications

Senia Paseta and Adrian Gregory (eds.), *Ireland and the Great War,* Manchester University Press

Terence Dooley, *The Decline of the Big House in Ireland,* Wolfhound Press.

Dorothy Macardle, *The Irish Republic,* Wolfhound Press

Joseph Lee, *The Modernisation of Irish Society 1848–1918,* Gill & Macmillan

Eoin Neeson, *Birth of a Republic,* Prestige Books

James Durney, *On the One Road,* Leinster Leader.

Patrick Murra y, *Oracles of God,* UCD Press

Desmond FitzGerald, *Memoirs of Desmond FitzGerald, 1913–16,* Routledge & Keegan Paul

Leon O'Broin, *Revolutionary Underground: The Story of the IRB, 1858–1923,* Gill & Macmillan

Senia Paseta, *Before the Revolution,* Cork University Press

Martin Mansergh, *The Legacy of History,* Mercier Press.

Angus Mitchell, *Casement,* Hans Publishing

Diarmuid Ferriter, *The Transformation of Ireland 1900–2000,* Profile Books

Padraig Yeates, *Lockout,* Gill & Macmillan

The Earl of Longford and T. P. O'Neill, *Eamon de Valera,* Gill & Macmillan

Michael Laffen, *The Resurrection of Ireland 1916–1923,* Cambridge University Press.

David FitzPatrick, *The Two Irelands,* Oxford University Press

THE WITNESSES

The following are the names and status (as given by themselves) of the witnesses whose statements relate to the 1916 Rising. Names marked * are witnesses whose statements were consulted by the author in the writing of this book

The abbreviations used are as follows:

InhÉ   Inghinidhe na hÉireann
ICA   Irish Citizen Army
CnmB   Cumann na mBan
FÉ   Fianna Éireann
IRA   Irish Republican Army
IRB   Irish Republican Brotherhood
ITGWU   Irish Transport and General Workers' Union
IV   Irish Volunteers

* Aloysius, Rev. Fr. OFM Cap, chaplain to 1916 leaders
* Augustine, Rev Fr. OFM Cap, friend of 1916 leaders
* Austin, John, observer of Battle of Ashbourne

* Barrett, Joseph, member IRB Clare, officer IRA
* Barry, Alice, Dr, friend of IRA leaders
* Barry, Leslie, member CnmB, wife of Tom Barry
* Blythe, Ernest, minister Dáil Éireann, 1921
* Booth, Frank, IRB Centre Belfast, member IV
* Boylan, Sean, captain IV Meath, member IRB
* Bracken, Peadar, member IRB, captain IV Tullamore
* Brannif, Daniel, member Dungannon Clubs,. member Supreme Council IRB, 1912–14
Brennan, Frank J., member IV Tullamore, 1916
* Browne, Rev Mgr Patrick, friend of Sean MacDermott, brother of Mrs Margaret MacEntee
* Bulfin, Eamon, Lieutenant IV, member IRB
Burgess, Alfred, brother of Cathal Brugha

* Brugha, Cathal, member IV
* Burke, Frank (Fergus), member IV Dublin, 1916
Burke, James, officer IV Dublin
Byrne, Bernard, member IV
Byrne, Gerarld (Garry), member IRB, IV and IRA
* Byrne, Tom, member Irish Brigade South Africa 1900–02, captain IV Dublin, 1916, commandant IRA, 1921

Caldwell, Patrick, member IV, 1916
* Callender, Ignatius, member IV Dublin, 1916
* Carpenter, Walter, member ICA Dublin, 1916
* Ceannt, Aine, bean Éamonn, widow of Éamonn Ceannt, executed 1916
Christian, William, member FÉ, member IV Dublin, 1916
* Clarke, Kathleen, widow of Tom Clarke, executed 1916
Cody, Sean, member IV Dublin, 1913–16
Cighlan, Francis X., officer IV Dublin, 1913–21
* Colbert, Elizabeth, sister of Con Colbert, executed 1916
* Colley, Senator Harry, officer IV Dublin
* Collins, Maurice, member IV and IRB
* Colum, Mary M., member CnmB
* Conlon, Martin, member Supreme Council IRB, 1916
* Connolly, Joseph, officer IV Belfast, 1916
* Connolly, Matthew, brother of Sean Connolly, member ICA, killed in action
Connolly, Richard, member Supreme Council IRB, 1916
Coughlan, James, member IV Dublin, 1916
* Cowley, Michael P., Centre IRB Dublin, 1908–16., assistant manager, National City Bank
Corrigan, William P., solicitor, member iv South Dublin Union Garrison, 1916
* Cosgrave, William T., member Marrowbone Lane Garrison, president Dáil Éireann, 1922–32
* Coyle, Eugene, Rev Canon, associated with IRB Tyrone, 1916
* Crean, Diarmuid, officer IV Kerry, 1913–14
Cremin, Michael, member IV Dublin, 1916, captain IRA, 1921
Crothers, Christopher, member ICA, 1916, member IRA 1920–21
Cusack, Dr Brian, member IV Dublin, 1916
Czira, Sidney, Mrs John Brennan, author, sister of Grace Gifford, officer CnmB

Daly, Denis, member IRB London, 1913
Daly, Francis, Centre IRB Dublin, 1908–16, assistant manager, National City Bank
Daly, Seamus, member IV and IRB Dublin, 1916
de Brun, Seosamh, member IV Dublin, 1916
* de Burca, Dr F., member IRB Dublin, 1916
Desborough, Albert George Fletcher, Lewis gun instructor, British army, Dublin, 1916
* de Valera, Éamon, B.A., Ph.D., commandant Bolands Mills, 1916. president Sinn Féin 1917–22. president Dáil Éireann 1919–22, an Taoiseach 1932–
Devine, Thomas, member IV Dublin, 1916
* Dillon, Geraldine, sister of Joseph M.Plunkett, executed 1916
* Dobbyn, Seamus, member Supreme Council IRB, 1916, 1917–21

Dolan, Edward, member IV and IRA Dublin, 1914–21

* Donnelly, Charles, member IRB and IV Rathfarnham, 1913–16

Donnelly, James E., captain IV Dublin, 1916

Donnelly, Nellie, née Gifford, sister of Grace Gifford,widow of Joseph M, Plunkett, executed 1916; member ICA

* Donnelly, Simon, captain IV and IRA Dublin, 1916–21

Doolan, Joseph, member IV Dublin, 1916

Dowling, Thomas, member IV Dublin, 1915–16

Doyle, James, survivor of Clanwilliam House Garrison, 1916, ASU1920–21

Doyle, John J., member IV Dublin, 1914–16, medical officer Dublin Brigade, 1917–22

* Doyle, Very Rev Patrick J., parish priest Naas, 1952

* Doyle, Peadar S., TD, officer IV Dublin, 1916

Doyle, Seamus, member IV Dublin, 1914–16, fought at Mount Street Bridge, 1916

Doyle, Thomas J., member IV Dublin, 1916

Duffy, Patrick, member IV Louth, 1916

Egan, Garda Patrick, lieutenant IV, 1916

Fahy, Frank, captain IV Dublin, 1916, member Dáil Éireann 1919–21, Ceann Comhairle Dáil Éireann, 1932–

Fitzgerald, James, officer IV and IRA Dublin, 1916–21

Fitzgerald, Theo, member IV and IRA Dublin, 1916–21

* FitzGibbon, Sean, member IV Executive, 1916

* Foran, James, member IV Dublin, 1916

Furlong, Major Joseph, IRB Wexford, 1908, IV London, 1913, IRA General Headquarters, 1920–21

* Gaskin, Frank, member IRB Liverpool, 1911, member IV, 1916

* Gavan-Duffy, Louise, sister of George Gavan-Duffy, secretary CnmB

* Gerrard, Captain E., British army officer in Dublin, 1916–21

* Ginnell, Mrs Alice, widow of Laurence Ginnell MP and TD

Gleeson, Joseph, member IRB Supreme Council, 1916

Gogan, Liam S., member IV Executive, 1916

* Golden, Gerry, member IV and IRA, 1916–21

* Grace, Seamus, member IV Dublin, 1914–16, fought at 25 Northumberland Road, 1916, officer IRA Dublin, 1921

* Hackett, Rose, member ICA, 1916

* Harris, Thomas, member IV Kildare

Hayes, Michael, Professor of Modern Irish, NUI, officer IV Dublin, 1916, member Dáil and Seanad, 1921, Ceann Comhairle Dáil Éireann, 1922–32

Hayes, Dr Richard, commandant IV Dublin, 1916, member 1st, 2nd and 3rd Dáil

Hehir, Hugh, member IRB and IV, 1911–16

Henderson, Frank, captain IV, 1916, commandant IRA, 1917–21

* Hennessy, Sean, member IV and IRA, 1916–21

* Heron, Archie, officer IV and IRA Dublin, 1916–21

Heron, Ina, daughter of James Connolly, member CnmB Dublin, 1916–21

* Heuston, John M. Rev Fr OP, brother of Sean Heuston, executed 1916

* Hobson, Bulmer, member IV Supreme Council, 1915, general secretary IV, 1916, founder FÉ, 1902
* Hobson, Clare, née Gregan, wife of Bulmer Hobson
* Holland, Robert, member IRB, FÉ and IV, 1909–16, member IRA, 1917–21

* Ingoldsby, Augustine (Gus), secretary Cumann na Gael, 1898
Irvine, George, member IRB and IV, 1907–16

Jackson, Valentine, Centre IRB Dublin, 1912
Joyce, Colonel J. V., officer IV and IRA Dublin, 1914–21

Kavanagh, Peter Paul, member IV Dublin, 1916
Kavangh, Seamus, member IV, 1916
* Keating, Mrs Pauline, member CnmB, 1915
Kearney, Patrick, member IV and IRA Dublin, 1913–21
Keegan, John, member IV Dublin, 1916
Kelly, Edward, member Hibernian Rifles Dublin, 1916, member Supreme Council IRB
Kennedy, Luke, member IV Executive, 1916
Kennedy, Margaret, member CnmB, 1916, senator, 1947–
Kennedy, Patrick, member ICA, 1916, member IRA, 1920–21
Kennedy, Sean, lieutenant IV Dublin, 1916, IRA, 1921
Kenny, James, lieutenant IV Dublin, 1916, IRA, 1921
Kenny, James, member IV and IRA Dublin, 1915–23
Kenny, Seamus, officer IV Dublin, 1916, member 1923–56
King, Martin, member ICA Dublin, 1916
* Knightly, Michael, member IV and IRA, 1916–21

Laffan, Nicholas, captain IV Dublin, 1916, captain IRA 1917–21
Lalor, Molly Hyland, executive CnmB
* Lawless, Michael J., member IV and IRA Dublin, 1915–21
Leahy, Thomas, member ICA Dublin, 1916
* Lennon, Michael J., member IV Dublin, 1916, District Justice 1937–57
* Little, Patrick J., Irish Representative in South Africa and South America, minister Dáil Éireann, 1939–48
Lynch, Diarmuid, member Supreme Council IRB, 1916
* Lynch, Fionan, member IV, 1916, member Dáil Éireann 1918–44, member Provisional Government, 1922, Circuit Court Judge, 1944–
* Lynn, Dr Kathleen, member ICA, 1916

* MacDonagh, Francesca, sister of Thomas MacDonagh, executed 1916
* MacEntee, Margaret, née Browne, wife of Sean MacEntee, courier to Galway, member of Cabinet, 1932–48
* MacEntee, Sean, officer IV and IRA, 1916–21, member of Cabinet 1932–48
MacGarry, Maeve, member CnmB, 1913–21
* MacNeill, Agnes, widow of Eoin MacNeill, chief of staff of IV; officer CnmB
MacBride, Maud Gonne, founder member Sinn Féin National Council and InhÉ
* McCabe, Kevin, member IRB, 1911, IV Dublin, 1914–16
McCartan, Dr Patrick, member Supreme Council IRB, 1916

McCarthy, Dan, member IRB and IV, 1913–16

* McCarthy, Thomas, captain IV Dublin, 1915

MacCarville, Eileen, captain University Branch CnmB Dublin

* McCullough, Denis, president Supreme Council IRB, 1916

MacDonagh, John, lieutenant IV, brother of Thomas MacDonagh, executed 1916

McDonnell, Michael, colonel, lieutenant IV, 1916

McDonagh, Joseph, member IV and IRA, 1916–21

McDowell, Mrs Maeve Cavanagh, member ICA, 1916

* McGallogley, John, member IRB Glasgow and Manchester, 1915, member IV Dublin, 1916, officer IRA Manchester, 1921

* McGarry, Sean, member Supreme Council IRB

McHugh, Patrick, lieutenant IV Dundalk, 1916

McLoughlin, Sean, officer IV 1916, organiser 1917

* McNamara, Rose, member InhÉ, 1906–12, member CnmB, 1913–22

McNeill, Josephine, Mrs, Officer CnmB, 1917–21, Widow of James McNeill Governor-General, Irish Free State 1928–34

* McQuaile, Charles S., member IV and IRA, 1913–21

* McWhinney, Linda, Officer CnmB, 1914–21

*Martin, Mrs Bridget, née Foley, CnmB 1913–16, courier to Cork 1916

Meade, Maurice, member Irish Brigade Germany, 1916, member IRA Limerick

* Meldon, Thomas J., member IV, 1915–20, officer IRA, 1921

* Molony, Helena, secretary InhÉ, 1907–14, member CnmB, 1915–21

* Monteith, Robert, IV 1913–15, associate of Roger Casement in Germany, 1915

* Moylett, Patrick, member IV, 1914

* Mulcahy, Richard, chief of staff IRA, 1919–21

Mulcahy, Mary Josephine, wife of General Richard Mulcahy, secretary CnmB, 1915–16, courier to Wexford, 1916

Mullen, Very Rev Patrick J., member IV, 1914–16

Murphy, Fintan, officer IV, 1914–16

* Murphy, Gregory, Centre irb Dublin, 1916, member IV and IRA, 1913–21

Murphy, John (Sean), member IRB Dublin, 1901, member IV Dublin, 1916

Murphy, Seamus, captain IV Dublin, 1914–16

Murray, Henry S., officer IV and IRA Dublin, 1914–21

Murray, Joseph, member IRB and IV, 1911–16

* Murray, Seamus, member IV Dublin, 1915–16

* Neligan, David, IRA intelligence agent in British Police Service

Nevin, Rev Fr Eugene, CP, chaplain to Marrowbone Lane Post, Easter 1916

Nicholls, Harry, captain IV Dublin, 1916

Nugent, Laurence, officer IV and IRA, 1913–21

O'Brien, Liam, member IRB and IV Dublin, 1912–16

* O'Brien, Annie, officer CnmB, 1916–21

O'Brien, Mrs Nora, née Connolly, member CnmB, daughter of James Connolly, executed 1916

Obroin, Padraig, member ICA, 1916

* O'Brolchain, Maire, vice-president InhÉ, member Sinn Féin

Ó Buachalla, Domhnall, member IV, 1913–16, last Governor-General of Ireland

O'Byrne, Joseph, officer IV, 1913–16. captain IRA Dublin, 1920

O'Byrne, Miss Maire Kennedy, member CnmB

* O'Carroll, Joseph, member ICA, 1916

O'Connor, John (Blimey), member Kimmage Garrison IV, 1916, IRA, 1919–21

* O'Connor, Joseph, IV second-in-command Bolands Mills, 1916, IRA, 1917–22

* O'Daly, Very Rev Canon James, member IRB Tyrone, 1916

* O'Daly, Major General Patrick, lieutenant FÉ, 1913–16, lieutenant IV, 1913–16,
ASU, 1920–21, lieutenant Irish Volunteers, 1913–16, IRA, 1921, member ICA

* O'Donoghue, Very Rev Fr Thomas, founder member FÉ, 1913–16

* O'Donovan, Con, B.Agr.Sc, member IRB, member IV and IRA Dublin

O'Donovan, Mrs Kathleen, sister of Harry Boland, killed 1922, wife of Senator
Sean O'Donovan

* O'Duffy, Sean M., lieutenant IV Dublin, 1916, organiser Republican Courts

O'Flaherty, Liam, member IV Dublin, 1916

O'Flanagan, George, member IV Dublin and IRA, 1916–21

* O'Flanagan, Michael, member IV and IRA, 1916–21

O'Hannigan, Donal, senior officer IV and IRA Dublin and Dundalk 1916–21

O'Hegarty, Patrick S., member Supreme Council IRB London and Dublin, 1902–16

O'Keeffe, Sean, officer IV, 1913–16

O'Kelly, J. J. (Sceilig), editor *Catholic Bulletin,* 1916

O'Kelly, Mairead, CnmB, 1913–16

* O'Kelly, Padraig, member IV Dublin, 1916

O'Kelly, Sean T., president of Ireland 1945–, took part in Rising 1916, Speaker
Dáil Éireann, 1920, Irish representative in Rome and Paris, 1920–21

O'Loughlin, Colm, captain IV, 1916, printer and publisher

Oman, William, member ICA, 1916

* O'Mara, Peadar, officer IV and IRA Dublin, 1916–21

O'Mullane, Bridget, Miss, officer CnmB, 1917

O'Neill, Edward, lieutenant IV, 1916

* O'Rahilly, Aine, CnmB, 1914–21, sister of The O'Rahilly, killed in action in 1916

* O'Reilly, Eily O'Hanrahan, CnmB 1914, sister of Michael O'Hamrahan, executed
1916

O'Riain, Padraig, secretary FÉ, 1916

O'Rourke, Joseph, Centre and secretary IRB Dublin, 1912–19

O'Shea, James, member ICA Dublin

* O'Sullivan, Seamus S., lieutenant IV, 1916

* Perolz, Marie, née Flanagan, InhÉ, courier Dublin, Waterford and Cork, 1916,
member ICA

* Plunkett, Grace, née Gifford, widow of Joseph Plunkett, executed 1916

Plunkett, John (Jack), brother of Joseph Plunkett, executed, lieutenant IV Dublin,
1916, lieutenant IV Dublin, 1916

* Pounch, Seamus, Fianna Dublin, 1916

Price, Major General Eamon (Bob), captain IV, 1913–16, IRA, 1920–21

Price, Sean, IRB, IV and IRA, 1915–21

* Pugh, Thomas, IV Dublin, 1916

* Reilly, Bernard, constable RIC Kerry, 1916, witness of arrest of Roger Casement
and seizure of *Aud*

* Ridgeway, Dr J. C. , British officer Dublin, 1916
* Robbins, Frank, member ICA, 1916, secretary ITGWU
Robinson, Seamus, officer IV 1916, IV and IRA Tipperary, 1917–21
Rooney, Catherine, née Byrne, CnmB, 1916
* Ryan, Desmond, lieutenant IV, 1916, author
* Ryan, Dr James, courier, took part in 1916, member Irish government, 1932–48
* Ryan, Mairín, née Cregan, wife of Dr James Ryan, minister, CnmB, 1913–21, courier Kerry, 1916

* Saurin, Lieutenant-Colonel Charles, member IV Dublin, 1914–16, officer IRA, 1917–21
* Saurin, Frank, IV, 1916, IRA, 1921 (intelligence)
Scollan, John Joseph, commandant Hibernian Rifles, 1916
Scully, Captain Thomas, member IV Dublin, 1916, IRA 1917–21
* Shelly, Charles, member IV Dublin and IRA, 1915–21
Shouldice, John F., Lieutenant IV Dublin, 1916, captain IRA, 1921
Slater, Thomas, member IRB Dublin, 1905, IV, 1915–16 IRA, 1917–21
Slattery, James, Col, IV Dublin, 1914–16, IRA, 1919–21
Slattery, Dr Peadar, Doctor, IV GPO, 1916
* Smart, Thomas, IV Dublin, 1915–16
Smith, Eugene, official in Dublin Castle, responsible for transfer of information to IV, 1913–18
Staines, Michael, IV 1913–16, quartermaster, member of Dáil Eireann, 1918–23, first Commissioner of Garda Siochána, 1923
Stapleton, William James, IV Dublin, 1913–19, IRA, 1921

Thornton, Bridget, Dr, née Lyons, CnmB Executive, 1918
* Thornton, Frank, IRB and IV Dublin, 1913–16, Intelligence, 1919–21
* Traynor, Oscar, captain IV, 1913-16, IRA, 1920–21
Twamley, John, IV, 1913–16

* Ui Chonaill, Eilis, née Ryan, member CnmB Executive

Walpole, Harry, IV Dublin, 1916
Walsh, James, IV Dublin, 1915–16, member garrison at Clanwilliam House, 1916
* Walsh, Thomas, IV Dublin, 1915–16, member garrison at Clanwilliam House, 1916
Ward, Patrick, Fiannna Eireann 1909 IV and IRA Dublin, 1914–21
* Whelan, William, IV Dublin, 1916, IRA England
* Wyse-Power, Charles, Judge, Member IV Dublin 1913, courier Limerick, 1916, counsel for defence of IRA prisoners
Wyse-Power, Dr Nancy, officer CnmB, 1914–16